JEFFREY BILHUBER

AMERICAN MASTER

Notes on Style and Substance

JEFFREY BILHUBER

AMERICAN MASTER

Notes on Style and Substance

FOREWORD BY MARISKA HARGITAY

Written by Sara Ruffin Costello
Photography by William Abranowicz

RIZZOLI
NEW YORK

New York Paris London Milan

THE LANGUAGE OF BEAUTY

Mariska Hargitay

"Beauty of whatever kind, in its supreme development, invariably excites the sensitive soul to tears."
— Edgar Allen Poe

Shortly after we had closed on our house, my husband and I were standing in our new living room, our minds full of ideas, brimming with the possibility and promise of a new home. We walked around the room, conjuring up seating arrangements and side tables and bookshelves, searching for all the right adjectives and descriptions for how we wanted it to look and feel. And then, in the same moment, we had a monumental idea that felt so right we didn't even need to say it: we would decorate the whole house ourselves. It made perfect sense! We'd had time to refine our taste, we knew what we liked, we had so many great pieces already, all we had to do now was figure out how to make it all fit together. I looked around the room, looked at Peter, and thought to myself, "Yeah, I think we got this."

Three days later, I was on the phone with Jeffrey: "Hi. Can you come over? Now?"

I had left a light-filled house in Los Angeles fifteen years earlier to come work in gritty, glamorous New York. Finding a new home base with decent exposures was a priority, and with a string of not-quite-right apartments in my wake, this sunny-ish spot, uptown and close to the park, finally felt like we had landed. Still, it was a tricky space. Specifically, it was the living room that stumped us. Not long after our intrepid decision to take on the task of decorating, I stood in that same living room and thought, "What are we going to do with this? This is a hallway. Why did we buy a hallway?"

That hallway was the reason for my lifeline call to Jeffrey. I had worked with him before, and, master of specificity that he is, the first thing he did was amend "hallway" to "bowling alley." On the first site visit to the house, he stood in the middle of my hallway/bowling alley/living room, with one hand on his hip and the other rubbing his chin (he stands like this when he's in creative mode), with a look that's somehow serious and playful at the same time, and proclaimed, "Mirrors! I see mirrors!"

Say mirrors to me, and I think Vegas hotel room. In the '80s. Not exactly what I was looking for. But I was willing to trust Jeffrey, because a conversation with him is always going to be a dialogue. He is a profoundly talented listener, with an ear for what clients are trying to express; he knows to ask the right questions, elegantly and expertly, the ones that will help tease out the personal clues that will guide his thinking. And, perhaps more simply, I trusted that if Jeffrey said mirrors, he had a good reason. Plus, I thought, what's wrong with a little Vegas?

And how did it all work out? Suffice it to say that when I stand in our living room now, I don't see a hallway. And I don't see a bowling alley. I see a triumph. (That's Jeffrey's word, and I love it.) The room is a triumph of light and space—and the most cunningly deployed mirrors I've ever seen.

When I first saw the mockups for *American Master*, my jaw just dropped. The book is so very beautiful, and so different. I love Jeffrey not only for his singular vision and the sophistication of his aesthetic, but for the breadth of his creative palette. I know many designers work with a tried and true formula of "here's what I do, now get on board," which can of course yield beautiful results. If you like what you see, you can simply say, "Yes, please do that to my house." But the thrill of working with Jeffrey is different. At the end of the project, you get the best version not of him, but of YOU.

When I described to Jeffrey what I wanted this house to be, I started with a simple word: fun. We have three children and I wanted to embed in their memories these beautiful recollections of a house that was steeped in play, down to the furniture. "When we were growing up," I picture them saying, "we had a purple couch! And an orange sofa!" I needed this house to be a home that made an impact on all of us who lived there, not just as a canvas on which we painted our memories, but a memory in and of itself. And we certainly didn't want the house to communicate "Now we are grown ups. And we're very serious. Please don't touch anything." I wanted the house to feel like anywhere the kids were, they could move things around, throw a couple of pillows on the floor, pile up and get cozy.

My favorite reaction to our house when people walk in now is "Mariska, this is *so* you!" It's the ultimate compliment to Jeffrey's skill, not only as a decorator, but also as a translator, because a home *must* feel personal.

I have always thought working with Jeffrey is a little like doing improvisation. The first rule of improv is to listen and react without preconceived expectations. We call it saying, "Yes . . . and"—instead of saying, "Yes . . . but." It's amazing what kind of unanticipated directions can open up when that little rule governs a creative discussion. Jeffrey and I could be talking about a simple detail, and one "yes . . . and" from one of us, and suddenly we're working a very interesting groove.

Jeffrey's affinity for improv came in especially handy because Peter and I weren't starting with a clean slate when we bought this house. We had pieces and objects from around the world that we didn't want to lose. It was important to us that Jeffrey repurpose—the fancy word for recycle—our things while adding new pieces. That chandelier I bought in 1999? That's the first piece I bought after moving to New York! That has meaning! These were all the little callbacks that gave us a deeper sense of belonging because they had made this journey. There were moments, when seeing what we already owned in the context of Jeffrey's new design, that would make us realize while a piece may have sentimental value, it's basically just old. That's when Jeffrey would deploy his inimitably elegant phrase, "I'm not sure that needs to be part of the decorative solution."

Another exciting aspect of working with Jeffrey is watching him distill an idea down to its essence. When Jeffrey was teasing out inspiration for how we wanted the house to feel, I also referenced my love for the beach. He translated that into a gorgeous, long sea-glass necklace, draped over the back of a chair in our living room. I once showed him a painting by Nancy Lorenz, all shimmery greens with inlaid pearl. I told him that I wanted the master bedroom to feel like that painting, like looking up at the sky from underwater. What he made was liquid cocoon, peaceful and safe, a watery sanctuary, and I couldn't love it more.

That kind of specificity, that kind of listening takes time, of course. And while we feel that our projects with Jeffrey have truly been collaborative, there comes a point where any master of a craft—because that's what Jeffrey is, a true master—must be left alone to do his work. That lesson hadn't quite sunk in when we were in the design process with this house. We had been out of town while Jeffrey was doing the installation, but we had one night in New York before heading out again, and in spite of Jeffrey's begging—"Please just wait, I want you to see it when it's done"—we walked in. And we hated it. The house was empty except for the new carpet and new wallpaper, both of which had made sense when he showed them to us—peacock blue and a very light caramel brown—but now, not at all. Peter sat with his head in his hands. "It looks like a doctor's office. A doctor who has a cousin in the carpet business. All that's missing are the Lucite magazine racks." I called Jeffrey's senior designer the next morning. "James, hi, look, I think we just made a terrible mistake. The carpet's not right and the wallpaper's not right. It's just not us."

James needs to be congratulated for not saying what he was thinking ("What part of 'Don't look at it before it's done' didn't you understand?") and answered, calmly and elegantly, "I'm so sorry to hear that. Why don't we just finish it and see how it goes. If you don't like it when it's finished, we'll see how we want to address it then."

Two weeks later, we walked back into the house and finally learned our lesson: don't peek over a master's shoulder while he is still working! What greeted us was, well, a triumph. Walking from room to room, we felt like we had been heard, like our happy history as a family was being honored, while at the same time, we were being offered an invitation to forge ahead into our next chapter. The house is mature, daring, playful—and beautiful.

After these many years of intimate collaboration with Jeffrey—literally sifting through my baggage together—I think I have a better understanding of his deep-seated drive to articulate himself through beauty, in the true sense of the word: "a combination of qualities, such as shape, color, or form, that pleases the aesthetic senses, especially the sight." Jeffrey's heart sings when his design answers our desire to see things in right relation to each other. Beauty is his way of ordering the world, his way of bringing order into our lives. I said working with Jeffrey is always a conversation. Indeed it is: he listens closely for how we define beauty, how we understand it, how he can create it for us, then he answers, in a language he has truly mastered.

THINKING BIG AND LOOKING FORWARD

Jeffrey Bilhuber

Our universal goal in life is to progress. I do believe every human being on the planet walks through their days with a sense of momentum directing his or her choices. As a decorator, my job is to be a glorious tour guide; to take your hand and lead you to inspired places where you have never been. As an artist, my responsibility is to define who we are and what makes the world that surrounds us modern. A world in which we are meaningfully attached and one that we can contribute to.

American Master represents years in the making—far more than the space between my last book and this. Through the lens of my long career, I want to share and exhibit the truisms of great style; not only an overview of materials and techniques, but maybe where our future just might be. The path I've been marching down the last few years has been to explore and pin down what makes us modern, and by better understanding that, we define ourselves and our time.

It takes a herculean effort every day to keep one's eyes open and pay attention to a changing world, and this remains the lifeblood of my work—a keen curiosity and a desire to see our world from all angles. Not to fall victim to a certain rhythm or others' expectations is always a colossal struggle no matter the project, but what I am continually testing for is uncommon ideas that inherently give us a modern sense of place and define our roles within that place. When new ideas work best, the client is whisked to another realm and is never quite able to look back at where they were with the same eyes. And this is precisely where I want to bring them.

In the past few months, for example, I have been bewitched by a collection of exquisitely spare tables manufactured from resin and sea salt that my workroom is commissioning for a client. Their forms are as modern as anything I have ever seen and absolutely connect to the moment that surrounds me. They are emblematic of an ongoing quest for newness. In fact, there isn't a room out there that can't be advanced by something new, in the same way that there is not a society that wouldn't benefit from an infusion of modernity through conversation and the sharing of ideas. It's a rapidly changing world and we need to be a part of it. As much as I can reference

"I know it will only be much later that people will realize to what extent the work I am doing today is in step with the future."
—Henri Matisse

with great self-assuredness our history and where we've come from, I'm most invigorated by where we are going.

I know my clients don't yearn for any other time and place. They crave today. At least the ones coming to me don't long for life in a different time, as though eighteenth-century France, for example, held more sway than now. There are many other successful designers who can build on that eighteenth-century perspective—but my clients want a taste of something they have not seen before. Although I may cull from the past, it's because I'm sampling what has already been test-driven and applying it to what we directly need to move forward. For the first time in many years, there is a very strong sense that everyone's looking to the future together and we want bright, forward-looking rooms to match that intrepidness.

In so much as I am breathing and working, I am a barometer of change. That's my job. Keeping current and staying in fashion means *to be in your time*. The gift of a creative mind and a relentless curiosity is a sort of wonderful burden that I wouldn't trade for anything. That ongoing battle within where primal forces push me to be better every time I go out; to be more inventive, to have more self-conviction, to raise the bar, to see the world with new eyes every day. It's an easy and dangerous thing to dine out on your laurels. You can become stagnant and fall behind if that's how you operate. When all my pistons are firing, I have understood my clients needs and encouraged them to find their voice, and in return they are exalted and their mood is not only reflected in their home, but out in the market as well. That's my responsibility!

As gratifying as the search-and-find missions are, as are the exploration of new relationships with artists, workrooms, and materials—it does require enormous backbone to take a stand for the unexpected. Even though I am as determined as an ox, there is fragility to the working component of the creative spirit. Presenting new ideas is not entirely dependent on having a receptive audience, but it is assisted by it. Anyone toiling in the creative field, whether it's designing or publishing or the fine arts or entertainment, is self-created and thrives with an audience. The audience gives them courage. The work needs it! I've found if I don't take care of my creativity and find a supportive and nurturing audience, it can be taken away. That is why I adore a well-tuned client-decorator relationship. The projects where we are both on the ride together flourish.

It takes great fortitude to convince someone of something unfamiliar. It's never easy. You give them the chance to accept, and if they don't you must be willing to move on. I truly believe if one idea doesn't lift off, there's another one right behind it. My great friend D. D. Ryan taught that to me, and D.D. learned it from another original thinker, Diana Vreeland. Give your ideas away—it makes room for more. It's important to know this! You go into a project thinking you've got to protect these sacred notions, but that's not at all the case—you release them and see where it can take you.

I wasn't always in a position to share my vision in a unique way. Back when I was still an undergraduate at the School of Hotel Administration at Cornell University (my first job was working the night shift as a housekeeper at the Carlyle Hotel!) I was so frustrated. I remember we were being instructed how to make muffins for five thousand people and I was the guy in the auditorium that kept raising his hand saying, "Are there any other options? Is this the answer, or *one* of *many*?" But that's simply what we were being taught: how to crank out sameness. I was in an industry that was teaching globalization and I wanted to be site-specific. I didn't understand that all hotels were supposed to look alike. I didn't understand that you must have the same experience in Lebanon as you had in Los Angeles. It just didn't make any sense to me. I believe regional indicators that identify where we are in the world and what we are supposed to do there, motivate us. Part of the reason I *had* to make the jump from the industry in which I was trained into the industry where I belong was this sense of responsibility to my voice. Ultimately, the real catalyst for leaving hospitality was a direct response to being told, "You can't do it like that!"

Dogma drives inventiveness. Hearing, "that's not the way it's done" or "you can't have those thoughts," is simply fuel that feeds my machine. That's not just my machine either; I think revolution is a fundamental human response. Similarly, I remember standing around at a social gathering as a young man. I wasn't contributing in a way that was expected. I was on the sidelines, lost in my own thoughts taking internal notes, when I overheard someone say, "Oh don't worry about Jeffrey, he's a wallflower." I thought, "Well . . . that's the end of that . . . that's done . . . I'll show you." And I've been off to the races ever since.

I'm hardwired to always want more, to go faster, and to achieve the most I can. That's the kind of drive that makes a great entrepreneur. There's a certain personality type that when they see the yellow light they slow down and wait for the red. I'm the type who speeds up and races to the green. At the end of the day, I'd like to be thought of as a leader, the alpha dog, not part of the pack, forging a trail versus following one.

I invite you to walk the trail with me. I promise you will be amazed by what I can show you, and you will never return to where you once were. You will have moved forward and life will never be the same.

TANGIER SUN WATER LILY MOON

The Palm Beach house ached for *a shock of the new* — confidence driven rooms that would lead the way, rather than follow a by-the-numbers approach. Since the client is well-traveled and has lived in very smart places, Bilhuber hatched a sublime design scheme to create an exotic atmosphere with gravitas, while simultaneously weaving in old world treasures, without using a drop of white. Anywhere. Period.

The foundation of the scheme started on the floor with a series of flat weave dhurrie carpets made to exact specifications in Bodhrum. Vivid colors with absolutely no pattern which Bilhuber laid out room by room. A saturated color scheme with a full spectrum followed: saffron, lemon, raspberry, plum, amethyst, eggplant, black cherry, lime, cerulean blue, blueberry, blue ink, navy, shocking pink, hyacinth, hibiscus, citrus, and tangerine. The paint on the walls is extraordinary, custom calibrated by Fine Paints of Europe with a viscous, dense composition. The colors were so clear and strong the painters thought Bilhuber might be completely mad. It was a bold gesture. They always are.

Bilhuber anticipated that his client—a worldly salon-iste—would regularly fill the sitting rooms of her numerous residences with a pastiche of clever personalities. Bilhuber's intention was to conceive an open plan of intimate groupings that would encourage lively discourse. A challenging furniture plan was worked and reworked until pleasing arrangements were presented—layouts which lean toward a traditional Eastern sensibility, with the furniture tucked into corners, opening up airy middle spaces. And all the while, composing new still lifes with beloved heirlooms. With the kilims, banquettes, and art finally in place, everyone was breathless with the ravishing results, including the once-skeptical painters.

OPPOSITE: **A bold color field oil on canvas by Ian Davenport hangs on citrus yellow walls in the stairwell and flawlessly encapsulates the pursuit of exotic color in this very snazzy Palm Beach casbah.**

OVERLEAF: **Backing away from a traditional furniture plan, the living room upholstery is tucked between columns and into corners to air out the middle. A close weave Indian ikat fabric spotlights the back-to-back serpentine chair. Black plum, duck egg blue, and citron green on the trim move the room's palette forward.**

Everything must register on one level or another. That's what details are for.

"Stingy bullion fringe makes me very sad," announces the decorator. "Drama is the whole point!" In other words, a beautifully crafted body should be finished accordingly. Gimp tape, contrast welting, tufted cushions, a box pleat, and, very often, *yards* of bullion fringe cascading three to four inches onto the ground, can be found adding zing to curtains, bells to sofas and whistles to armchairs in Bilhuber's world.

Bullion, which is made up of thick silk roping covered with threads of fine gold or silver, is usually reserved for staid Edwardian interiors. However, the thick braid of bullion running around the base of the divan in the picture opposite acts as a dramatic device, re-channeling this breezily alluring Palm Beach living room by adding heft, sumptuousness, and civility. Bullion is so much beloved by the decorator it actually skirts the edge of the mantle piece at his country house, Hay Fever, as a sort of smoke screen—as far and wide as this writer has traveled in the interior design world, that particular decorating gambit has never been witnessed! It is precisely these details—refined wisps punctuating rooms—that really matter because they serve to magnify the vitality of the whole.

Early in Bilhuber's career, Givenchy introduced him to close friend Bunny Mellon as he thought they might like to work together. It was decided Bilhuber would join them for dessert after the two had lunch at La Cote Basque on 53rd Street. At the meeting, the young decorator was struck by their close bond. The two strong personalities shared a mutually creative alliance circling around simplicity and refinement. Bilhuber remembers, "They fed off each other in the most admirable way." As the three were leaving, Mellon spotted her blue Mercedes station wagon waiting across the street, but Givenchy was having trouble finding his own driver. "Let me help you Hubert," she said, "What color is your car?" "It is a Silver Lincoln," he replied. She leapt in the street, flailing her arms to wave down the approaching vehicle. The car slowed, but then sped up. Givenchy looked at her, "Bunny, I said silver, that was *pearl grey*."

It's the details that matter.

OPPOSITE: **Bullion fringe cascades three inches off the bottom of the divan. This flourish dramatically finishes a look made up of framboise colored seat cushions, a printed linen stripe covering the frame, and then edged with a cut from the same fabric, run horizontally. Next to this abundance of upholstery, the appropriate choice is a bony pair of antique gilded Moroccan chairs with boxed tangerine cushions.**

PREVIOUS SPREAD: Window trim picked out in citron lime and duck egg blue, alongside embroidered matchstick shades, echoes the peregrine mood of the house. Scaled-up art lines the walls in the stairwell. On the left a Valery Koshlyakov odalisque made of packing tape in the image of *The Bather* by Ingres, and a Dominic Harris three-dimensional light box on the right.

OPPOSITE: Covered in a hand-painted paisley, a deeply tufted banquette smacks old-fashioned associations away, though the lilac leopard chair winds up being the star you can't take your eyes off.

OVERLEAF: In the dining room, just off the Moorish colonnade that runs the length of the house, an existing panoramic mural is reduced to a mere background element (as it was intended to be) by a super-scaled oak leaf painting by Chester Arnold that acts as a giant magnifying glass. Behind green Moroccan fretwork, is a tangerine back panel adding a mosaic of animation. What makes the room work, however, is an upholstered armchair that counteracts the leggy-ness of all those Regency seats. A solid cobalt blue dhurrie carpet controls the chaos.

I adore one powerful, stirring concept as a catalyst to help me create.

Too often decorators are asked, "What was your inspiration? What wild fire lit this procession of color and pattern?" It's a vexing question for a designer. The answer is usually amorphous—creative synapses firing all together in the middle of the night. It's impossible to explain honestly.

Inspiration, for Jeffrey Bilhuber, is approached with complete volumetric immersion—everything all at once, and simultaneously put through a sieve. Like panning for gold in a turbulent stream, the sparkle will eventually surface. It usually begins with a rush of hazy images: a dark chocolate soufflé on a black marble counter at a country house, snazzy dialogue from a long ago dinner at a Moroccan restaurant in Manhattan, a hooked carpet from a venerable old American rug shop, a stylish client's light-up lucite clutch sitting on the table at a meeting, the emotional feeling of a certain decade, iconic rooms seared into memory, the physical library of upholstery shapes and fabric memos back at the office and design studio. Sometimes solidifying a concept is as linear a chemical process as liquid forming into ice. Sometimes not.

Iconoclast French designer Hubert de Givenchy, recognizing a spark in Bilhuber, took a gamble and hired the fledgling decorator to spiff up his design studio and atelier on 75th and Madison, then across from the Whitney Museum. As he was giving Bilhuber a tour of the space, Mr. Givenchy gazed out the window to look at the Whitney—a brown chunk of a building which Bilhuber had always thought of as severe, even ugly—and suggested, "They should light it at night, it would be a beautiful sculpture." In one moment, Givenchy had recast the museum's Brutalist architecture, seeing the possibility for beauty in its simple presence, intimating, "Look again, Jeffrey. See with new eyes."

Overcooked design tropes are taboo at Bilhuber and Associates. "Mixing and matching" are dirty words. Working out different muscles with each project is essential to the fitness of the work. The designer and his team prefer the painful approach which means a certain amount of hand wringing, and can-we-really-pull-this-off panic.

It all starts with open eyes. Overlooked chairs and unconventional upholstery shapes are lassoed out of the crowded decorating corral and used to build new paradigms for each project, producing rooms that make us sit up and say, "Would you look at that!" The writer David Foster Wallace captured the essence of possibility when he addressed Kenyon College graduates at a commencement speech: "What really matters is being conscious and aware enough to choose what to pay attention to." If you aren't alert, you can miss the opportunity that's right in front of you.

As Bilhuber wrapped up the initial Givenchy site visit, scribbling in his notebook the entire time, he finally asked, "So, what's the look we are going for?" Givenchy's response, "I want it to look like a bird's nest." An image so powerful for Bilhuber that it set into motion the entire visual narrative. That one stirring concept was the golden ring: a schematic direction for the atelier, but in the longer view, Givenchy had provided Bilhuber with a new lens through which to see the world, recognizing the power of beauty in anything.

OPPOSITE: **An antique pedestal-based dining table sits in front of a cushy banquette whose gilded and ebony flash of carved legs provide yet another detail to savor. The cove ceiling, rather than just evaporating into blue sky, is instead painted like an amethyst canopy.**

Place interesting objects next to each other and they will tell a compelling story.

Bilhuber is a master storyteller. Someone for whom remembering historical dates, names of obscure books, and random lines from theatrical releases isn't a problem. He can easily grab his audience from go and then release them with a satisfying wallop, tossing in spicy details along the ride. Curating is similar to a well-told story in that carefully selected objects are positioned next to related content to support a thesis. In the same way varying tempo and modulation captivates the listener, still lifes too, must whisper or shout depending on the situation. Juxtaposing timeless and timely pieces like an animated pair of Venetian glass blackamoors and a teal glazed Chinese porcelain lamp, arranged below contemporary art produces a grand narrative — one that's a bit foreign, a little academic, and very civilized.

You would think most decorators would prefer to start with a tabula rasa in order to control the story. Not Bilhuber. He would rather receive directional indicators that issue from the client. Personal mementos and sentimental furniture are the clues that make the story richer and ultimately make the homeowner's heart soar. Perhaps for this fundamental reason Bilhuber's projects uniquely differ from one another because they tend to represent the client's real life as well as the decorator's vision. Even the sleekest minimalist adores having a prized possession show up somewhere in the newly installed apartment. Including memento mori is the difference between a home with a beating heart or a home with a flatline.

This attuned process never supersedes the importance of editing, however, and, decorating rule number one still remains: first edit, then curate. "You tend to feel old-fashioned when you are burdened with too much furniture or too many objects," explains the decorator. Removal is a *wonderfully* cathartic process. Letting go of shabby props that have been hanging around for decades is a huge relief. In a way, you don't lose anything, you just gain what matters.

PAGES 26-27: **Referencing the shadowy mystery of the Far East, matchstick shades, hand-embroidered in India with cotton thread, filter the exterior light. Upholstery is dressed in rich spice market solids, while the deeply tufted Chesterfield sofa wears a cloak of silk crewelwork.**

PREVIOUS SPREAD: **Saffron perforated curtains keep the eye focused inward on details like an English table with a muscular apron and a needlepoint cover. Amidst the traditional elements, a graphic grid painting by Carlos Estrada-Vega energizes the arrangement.**

OPPOSITE: **Spring boarding off the tropical green hue outside the window, moss-colored combed resin gives body to the space and immerses the garden room in organic color just neutral enough for the coral chair, raspberry pillow, and saffron curtains to sing. The framed oil on canvas painting is by Alfred Jensen.**

OPPOSITE: An edited collection of furniture, culled from the client's previous homes, steeps the Palm Beach house in the owner's history. Portiere curtains screen the garden room from the adjacent kitchen, giving the cook a bit of privacy. A Chuck Close painting and a Tom Holland enameled screen bring new worlds together with the helpful eye of an articulate and discerning collector.

OVERLEAF: A creamy hand-blocked wall covering set off by tangerine lacquer trim, references the pageantry in other rooms, but allows a bit of an exhalation. A Lisa Milroy butterfly painting hangs above a plum lacquered table whose eggshell satin finish quietly settles the room.

LEFT: **A gilded bullseye mirror and a bombé-formed table loaded with Chinese porcelain peaches, are repurposed from the client's other residences, but mixed together anew to create an exhilarating tablescape in the master suite.** OPPOSITE: **A discreetly Moorish headboard suggests an Eastern top note next to a traditional English bedside table. The small oil on canvas landscape is a surprise, like a porthole window picking up the gilt on the lamp and painted Moroccan footstool.**

You're only as good as your client.

If you ask the decorator, "How on earth did you dream this one up?" he will often credit his collaborator saying, "I had the BEST client."

The client/decorator relationship is loaded with mutual responsibility. No one hires Jeffrey Bilhuber with the idea of second guessing every decision; he is brought onto a project precisely because of his vision, experience, and leadership. On average, most jobs require a year from start to finish with all hands on deck working furiously, meticulously, and creatively toward the grand and final install. The best results always come from taking the plunge together, while still allowing the decorator a particular type of freedom that encourages him to lead the way to the best possible outcome devoting 110 percent of his skill set to that project. Bilhuber doesn't aim to meet expectations, he sets his sights on exceeding them!

The Palm Beach house was enlivened by such a relationship. The client—a confident, articulate, enthusiastic, and energetic woman with a strong point of view who encourages the same from those with whom she surrounds herself—brought an enormous wealth of ideas and knowledge to the table. She's worldly and aware, the way a devoted traveler must be. She is strategic, organized, and entertains with creativity and care, so the house had to be decorated to complement her admirable salon-iste perspective. Bilhuber points to a series of communications sent from the homeowner to him sporadically during the creative process, written completely in purple (or amethyst, or aubergine) and ALL CAPS, which he lovingly refers to as "the eggplant email updates." Bilhuber lived for and loved these missives, "They empowered me to be better, to exceed expectations, to dream."

A glorious exchange of ideas was established where decisions were made quickly. The homeowners expected a vibrant, culturally inclusive atmosphere that would ultimately come to reflect what it means to be modern today. As a result of the contributions of a trusting client, these rooms not only function marvelously, but also radiate energy, personality, and beauty. As Bilhuber would say, "A great actor is only as good as his audience."

PREVIOUS SPREAD: Part of a suite of bedrooms outfitted with a range of Indian hand-blocked fabrics, the second floor sitting room's Napoleonic chairs are brilliantly restored and recovered, with their nineteenth-century bead trim intact.

OPPOSITE: The library office windows are unusually dressed in a Brandolini print with tall panels situated on either side of a valence which is hung on the inside, rather than on the face, as is custom. Citron green tape running up the leading edge is designed to move your eye vertically up the wall, disguising a window that didn't rise to the occasion of the high ceilings.

THE DEVELOPED EYE

OPPOSITE: In the de Gournay swathed master bedroom, a peacock called George gazes perpetually at himself in a handmade convex oyster shell mirror designed by ceramist, Eve Kaplan.

OVERLEAF: Methodically stacked pictures support the scholarly mood of the drawing room, while gilded frames and gold fillet around the ceiling help animate the light.

Bilhuber's Manhattan apartment is the apotheosis of the decorator's career. Its rooms possess the strong personality of their creator; design meted out with equal measures of correctness and charm. The sum of its parts adds up to a kind of luxurious remove. A ritzy escape pad in a tough city. Referencing New York's Gilded Age, the period from 1868 to 1900, the apartment exudes the curiosity of a period in American history marked by intellectual growth in the arts and sciences, as well as economic expansion. One is reminded of the lively atmosphere of private clubs like the Lotos and the Union League—elegant backdrops for swells to meet and hash out railroad investments or discuss the latest Sargent exhibition. At the same time in Europe, an era of decadence and beauty was pulsing along. The Belle Epoque in Paris produced the Eiffel Tower, the Gare d'Orsay, and Paul Gauguin. Bilhuber samples from both those exuberant aesthetic movements, but the translation is fluent twenty-first-century American urban allure.

Every project involves historical culling, and it is through that sampling that the decorator paves a path toward tomorrow. Only a master who has had years of experience drilling down deep into the landscape of our past, is able to enlighten the marketplace with his developed vision, and therefore to articulate modernity. The apartment in this chapter exists on one level as Bilhuber's private refuge for family and friends, and on another, as a design laboratory where his creativity and his quest for new and ever better solutions are tested. Where are we going? How do we define the world around us? How do we reflect the society in which we live? The answers to these questions drive Bilhuber's work, and fuel the master's work ethic. Curiosity is what gets Bilhuber bouncing out of bed every morning, hitting the streets with purpose. His thoughtful response can be found in each and every project in this book.

Rooms should reveal themselves gradually over time.

Bilhuber's Manhattan apartment is the apex of his decorating prose—a sublime mixture of the colloquial and the recondite. An arrangement of curated sentences: some places you need to pull out a dictionary and others are meant to move the story along.

Born from a curiosity about New York's Gilded Age, the designer scrupulously studied the city's nineteenth-century architecture, especially the profoundly beautiful period rooms, miraculously still intact, at the Seventh Regiment Armory on Park Avenue. Sampling from the lavish dialogue of the Herter Brothers (the venerable interior design firm who decorated for the Vanderbilts and was also responsible for the White House under Ulysses S. Grant back in the late 1800s) and Louis C. Tiffany, Bilhuber muscles through a grab bag of Aesthetic Movement silhouettes, including Renaissance Revival, Art and Crafts, and Anglo-Japanese styles. But he does not leave it there. That would be too one-note, too reductive—and this is the full Bilhuber opera.

While the author's chief thesis is luxe, historical academia—the backbone of the story belongs to the animation of light. Bilhuber has wrapped the ceilings with gilded and carved fillet moulding, capturing the sun's rays and allowing them to dance around the edges of the room.

On the subject of filleting, there is an astonishing design footnote to that famous English house, Chatsworth, which Bilhuber will point out if you ever get him going on the topic of harnessing light. Did you know that all the *exterior* sashes on the windows at Chatsworth are gilded? In other words, the outside windows are leafed with gold. In fact, the Dowager Duchess of Devonshire, who clearly had the Midas touch (her small apartment at the vicarage featured fillet as well), had them re-gilded when they had started to crack and dim. If you see a picture of Chatsworth in the late afternoon, it appears to be fully aglow on the landscape—a beacon of civilization, the footprint of democracy. What an appropriate idea in a landscape that tends to be in a haze of dense green most of the time.

At the end of the day, it's the gilding that supports the narrative in a linear way. Around picture frames, on small animated stencils of copper leaf on the wallpaper in the dining room, and even splashed with a contemporary fling by artist Nancy Lorenz across the de Gournay panels in the bedroom; all those touches of gold allow the minor characters—like eglomise tie-backs and cloisonné lamps—to become suddenly alert, revealing personalities in full bloom. Genius.

PREVIOUS SPREAD: **The cosseted environment is set off by a Belle Epoque suite of furniture covered in original gros point needlework and damask. Crimson tones are threaded through with indigo and emerald, which appear on the cloisonné lamp and velvet sofa at opposite end.**

OPPOSITE: **The success natural candlelight brings should not be overlooked. Flanking the central mirror, are wall mounted Directoire sconces whose purple candles actually get lit every evening.**

OVERLEAF: **A room of one's own to work, or in this case, a magnificent Carlton desk with raised sides for privacy, and a twentieth-century bronze and champlevé floor lamp topped with pagoda fringed shade, positions the drawing room as a fine spot for writing important notes. Above the desk, a nineteenth-century academic plaster mold.**

PRECEDING LEFT PAGE: **A** stimulating palette of amber moiréd walls, red damask, and eggplant colored window treatments (with headers of pomegranate bullion fringe) are accented by the intricate patterns of the cloisonné lamp base and verre eglomise curtain tie back.
PRECEDING RIGHT PAGE: **A** contemporary **Chuck Price** sculpture perches atop one of a pair of heavily carved seventeenth-century brackets that are positioned to heighten the elevation, drawing the eye up.

OPPOSITE: **Art** is stacked counter-intuitively—a deeply saturated Dutch landscape is installed at standing height, bracketed by a larger work on paper above and a diminutive plaster bas-relief below.

Skip to the loo . . .

Everyone should have a smashing powder room. As germane to the concept of saying "I'm happy that you are here!" as a beautifully scented entrance hall or a well-stocked guest bedroom are, the powder room ought to be treated as another opportunity to flex one's hosting skills. It doesn't take much to max out a small room either: a bit of extraordinary wall covering, handsome hardware, an interesting mirror, and flattering lighting can rapidly transform a tiny space. Additionally, since the guest bathroom is a private refuge, it's an appropriate landing spot for more intimate gestures like sketches tucked into the mirror that would be lost in more formal locations.

For Bilhuber, powder rooms are a significant aspect of every client-decorator conversation because it's a chance to expand the decorative solutions already in place. The established tone of the house can be emphasized or amped up in the bathroom: dense color, ravishing wallpaper, honed marble, eglomise glass, amber lighting whatever the direction—it's simply marvelous to open the bathroom door and discover a little luxury. It is here that freshly pressed hand towels (especially the HUGE antique versions with impressive monograms!) and sweet smelling soaps finally get their golden opportunity to be of use. In fact, why not tuck a few stems of sweet peas into a small and stunning vase while you're at it?

Bunny Mellon combined the BEST of both worlds when she banished hand towels altogether at Oak Spring Farm in Virginia. In its stead were enormous lemon scented geraniums whose velvet soft oily leaves were used to dry, scent, and moisturize your hands as you ran them across the plant after washing up.

A client of Bilhuber's who is a couture icon uses her powder room in New York to display a collection of sketches and photographs of her! These are wonderfully personal pieces of art created by various friends in fashion and given to her over the years that tell the story of her life. You could spend an hour in that room studying her work through the decades. Unrestricted personal effects like these allow visitors a glimpse of what matters to you and are a welcomed companion to more public art found around the rest of the house. Bilhuber will often use the powder room for precisely this kind of personal statement—scrapbooking writ large. The modicum of effort required in designing a pleasing W.C. for you and your guests will be returned tenfold with every satisfying trip to it!

PRECEDING LEFT PAGE: **The drawing room is an education in perfection without coldness. Like a warm embrace from someone you admire, it's a restorative room that facilitates your best conversation.**

PRECEDING RIGHT PAGE: **Since the apartment's orientation is on an East West axis, the quality of the light changes from glorious canary white to amber gold and finally to a deep cognac.**

OPPOSITE: **Mauny flocked wallpaper in "salon vert" colorway and a nineteenth-century Italian mirror liner set inside a shadow box, align the powder room with the splendor of the adjacent drawing room. Postcards from a Sargent exhibition, as well as other mementos, create a wonderful distraction from peering too closely at one's own reflection.**

OVERLEAF: **Everything about the breakfast room is meant to coddle. Western facing exposures filter the sun, waking up Mauny's French nineteenth-century block print pattern wallpaper whose copper rosettes gently reflect the daylight. Every morning a pressed Irish linen tablecloth is laid over the green billiard cloth (baize) where the family religiously gathers for the first meal of the day.**

JOHANN CHRISTOPH BILHUBER

Curtains do something to a room!

Bilhuber *adores* dressing windows. With the range of a seasoned fashion designer who lives to drape cloth, his original creations are one of the distinctions of his design studio. If there were just one thing you could buy off the rack from his workroom, it would be a collection of Bilhuber prêt-à-porter window treatments.

But frankly, which type of curtain and in what material are decisions best left to the master. For example, a flouncy silk festoon shade with a tassel cord is appropriately black tie, but when executed in a casual block print, it becomes antidotal to formality.

Assessing the practical and decorative needs of a house requires an experienced eye, especially when it comes to yardage of hand-loomed cloth that can certainly "tip the scale." Loaded with an encyclopedic knowledge of what works where, Bilhuber might breezily reference a sheer treatment from an obscure book like Peter Thorton's, *Authentic Décor*, and riff on that. Certain situations call for classic architectural fixes like portiere curtains, a type of draping dating back as early as the second century, that strategically delineate a space. In other instances, windows might stagger unevenly across the side of a room and require balance. For that dilemma, Bilhuber would fool the eye with a series of sheer panels across the middle and fixed panels of a different fabric at either end, which effect one large window in a boldly modern way. Another sneaky trick to remedy the dead wall space between the top of a window and a high ceiling is to hang panels from just below the ceiling moldings, with a valance on the *inside* rather than the outside. Short windows now look like a tall drink of water as that outside panel leads the eye up vertically and the inside valence cuts horizontally like a shade.

Curtains have a duality; their primary function is to block the light and secondarily, they ought to dazzle. Like Scarlett O'Hara, you should have a vague desire to rip them off the wall and wear them.

PRECEDING LEFT PAGE: **With a wink to a Horst photograph of Baron de Rothschild's foot—wearing a floral embroidered slipper—standing on an intricate Savonnerie carpet, Bilhuber positions a noir needlepoint armchair against patterned Mauny wallpaper.** PRECEDING RIGHT PAGE: **Gold leaf compotes that might be used for stewed fruit and crème Anglaise, jockey for shelf space with decanters of bourbon and distilled water.**

OPPOSITE: **Decorative substance begins with form and ends with function: a block print festoon shade is raised and lowered by a large silk tassel that operates the chord mechanism.**

Rooms can be successful but still remain flat—that's when you add horsepower.

The bedroom had been installed and the de Gournay panels hung. At some defining point after the install, it became clear that another decorative step was needed. Something irreverent, modern, and responsively reactive.

What was required was a dose of youthful energy. At the eleventh hour, the decorator brought in his secret weapon, contemporary artist Nancy Lorenz, to dial the decor *up*. Waking up the walls with a fearless splash of gold-painted resin across the chinoiserie, Lorenz's small, bright note of modernity invigorated the place a hundred fold. It should be noted that this was the *first* and *last* time Lorenz did a site-specific commission. It was tough. It hadn't been done before, but it was worth it. It invigorated a room and cemented their relationship!

In the same spirit, Bilhuber clients Trey and Jenny Laird approached the decorator about designing their seminal house in Marfa, Texas. The mission was simple: keep it clean and modern, design responsibly, and create a house that fits the goals of the community. Marfa is a small town in the West Texas panhandle that blossomed under the guidance of Donald Judd and the founders of the Chinati Foundation, which was created to present and preserve an important group of contemporary artists' work devoted to site specificity and the landscape. It became a project that pushed all its participants, owners, architects, designers, gardeners, and builders to reassess what they have created before and set their sights upon new goals. The Lairds are influencers with a creative pedigree; Trey's firm, Laird + Partners, has charted new courses for fashion and beauty brands like Karl Lagerfeld, Donna Karan, and Rimmel, among others over the years. When the couple requested a totally new take on Texas, the decorator delighted in cranking up the nowness, knowing that out-of-the-box ideas would be encouraged. Amping up the emotional surprise (with a reverential nod to Yves Saint Laurent and Pierre Bergé in Marrakesh), graphic African mosaic tiles were folded into a series of white rooms with sandblasted floors. The results are exciting, exotic, and fresh. Rather than trodding a familiar path toward modernity, and with the encouragement and enthusiasm of Jenny and Trey, Bilhuber re-routed, taking a different road, bringing new elements along the way. The Lairds' house—a project still underway—tips its hat to previous Marfa trailblazers like artists Donald Judd and John Chamberlain, while thoroughly exhibiting the fearless personality of its owners. The fuel to add horsepower to the project was in direct response to being sensitive and articulate to a world that's in a constant state of change. The "newness" is a reaction to the nowness that matters most to those creative people at the forefront of design and the arts, and how it influences and affects us all.

OPPOSITE: There is something ritualistic and soothing about the atmosphere a wall-hung clock bestows. Wound every seven days, the audible tick-tocking settles the house admirably, in time and place. Otherwise, the entrance hall is a nod to Istanbul's Topkapi Palace where surface treatments and ornament mesh together.

OVERLEAF: Course linen hopsacking hung in the foyer and fixed to one side, is a tempering measure amidst the louche expanse of crimson wool velvet Wilton carpet connecting the rooms of the gallery.

PAGES 70-71: An arabesque armchair by master artisan John Henry Belter (known for his magnificent Rococo Revival furniture) anchors a corner of the bedroom. Phantom or jib doors, of which there are seven in total, allow the de Gournay scenic wall covering to surround without interruption.

LACQUERED LIFE

Late one night the decorator was in the midst of rapid and successive e-mails with his client discussing the project, "But how do you want it to *feel?*" asked Bilhuber, "What is the defining word we're looking for with this astonishing house?" They danced round and round style concepts—sending each other visuals that might apply and big ideas they hoped to incorporate. And then suddenly, there it was, one pivotal notion to launch the project: "I've got it!" Bilhuber wrote, "Sybaritic!" Sometimes just one strong word can drive all the decorating decisions.

The impact of that midnight conversation was that decorator and client developed a meaningful and true vocabulary for the house. From those touchstone words, Bilhuber was able to craft sentences and paragraphs until a compelling story started to unfold. Every hand-wringing design decision thereafter was poked from different angles: does it support our narrative? Will it move the story forward? When you are spinning a good tale, it's evident what bits will drive momentum and what bits need to be edited out.

Everything about this period Manhattan townhouse feels like a voluptuous embrace. Built out to fully support the pleasure thesis, the decorator installed sumptuous wool carpets across the floors, hand-loomed cloth on all the bench-made upholstery, and a jaw-droppingly original mural made from abalone shell, plaster, and lacquer that adorns the bay window of the main living room. Bilhuber included flocked wallpaper that makes you want to caress it, smoothly lacquered walls that pull the light from the windows at either end toward the middle, and enhanced trims and frames in a spectrum of color. It's all the Bilhuber pizzazz in five vertically stacked floors of ravishing beauty.

The decorative solutions throughout the house reveal a well-told story, but in a bigger sense, it is design that assists the lives and informs the memories of its inhabitants. When the house was installed, exactly eight months to the date later, what emerged were a series of seductively luxurious rooms that simply command you to immerse yourself in the sybaritic experience. From the get-go, the homeowners were angling for an enormously hospitable, unpretentious house. What they got was an expression of their true selves: a fearless, pleasure-loving, tour de force of polished design and pure joy.

OPPOSITE: **A classical presentation turned inside out redirects our attention in a modern way; the outside back and arm of a pair of bergères is covered in traditional cotton floral while the inside is done in yellow leather, trimmed with a splendid red gimp. The Spanish 1930s carpet, originally palace-sized and reconfigured to fit wall-to-wall, enhances the volume of the living room.**

OVERLEAF: **A digital super-graphic mounted on the wall in the foyer is a calculated preview in anticipation of the drama beyond. This is a modern device used to great effect that overlaps technology and the designer's craft.**

What's liberating is to be fearless.

Boldness arrives at a project because someone has taken a leap of faith. The client, that's who. When, for example, the decorator suggests that the central architectural focus of the room, a bay window, be lacquered in a myriad of colors to resemble an eighteenth-century Spanish high bas-relief screen, the client as well as all the tradespeople involved, must exhale and say, "We trust you. Lead the way!"

The townhouse featured here is cued from this one breathtaking design leap. To pull off the mission, Bilhuber relied on the unflappable skill of his chief lacquer artist, at whom almost any out-there idea can be flung. First, there are interpretations of pages and pages of inspiration. Next painted boards must be reviewed and tested to see that the structure will be sound. A laborious process of layering color upon color follows: the impasto build-up of the surface, the encrustation of crushed abalone shell, the meticulous application of gold leaf with a badger-hair brush. This series of actions requires a leader and a decision maker, which is precisely why the homeowner hired the decorator in the first place; they have brought in the big guns, complete with back office support.

Townhouses in Manhattan typically hoard precious light at either end. The interior designer is challenged with pulling that light through, and illuminating the darker middle areas. Killing two birds with one bright stone, Bilhuber not only endorsed the bay window's architecture by painting it like a contemporary trompe l'oeil screen, but also reinforced the light coming through it with a lacquered finish applied to all the interior walls. The painted bay creates a forced perspective that, when you walk through the middle door leading out to the terrace, feels like you are walking right through the center of a painting. A marvelous moment that gives back ten-fold what it took to put in.

With a game client, a talented backup crew, and a strong leader, the trust flows in an infinite circle. That's when projects soar.

PREVIOUS SPREAD: A voluptuous space meant to carry you away, the living room's furniture plan is driven by social aspects; a skirted hexagonal center table is used for entertaining and doubly reinforces the shape of the bay window whose center door opens out to the garden. Glassy, yolk yellow lacquered walls reflect animated light inside, where townhouses tend to be dark.

OPPOSITE: Referencing legendary nineteenth-century French lacquer artisan Jean Dunand, the enchanting bay window mural is finished with a combination of plaster, raised lacquer, abalone shell, and gold, platinum, and silver leaf to interpret Bilhuber's vision of a painted folding screen.

OVERLEAF: A narrow Manhattan room width dictates lower shapes in the center and higher silhouettes along the edge. Covered in tweed upholstery from haute loomer Toyine Sellars, interpretations of nineteenth-century slipper chairs are tweaked to be deeper and wider and sit closer to the floor. Louis Seize commissioned banquettes, upholstered in luxe handmade fabric from Tara Chapas, bookend the chimneybreast where a pair of formal cobalt blue Jasperware lidded urns are given pride of place.

PAGES 82–83: A deceptively simple visual device meant to diffuse the saturation of the yellow lacquered walls, the decorator tosses a single pillow of the same hue amidst pink and blue on the living room sofa.

I like anything that requires detailed, creative attention, especially lampshades.

At exactly 12:30 on a spring day, the designer received an unexpected call from Anna Wintour, a client and friend. A dash to the phone followed: "Hi Jeffrey, it's Anna. My lunch was cancelled and I'd love to see some lamps."

"Wonderful!" Bilhuber replied, "Let me know where you are and I'll meet you before we head off." Wintour replied, "Please don't worry about me. I know how busy you are, and this is completely unplanned. Just let me know the name of a shop or two and I'll dash over and take a look." Pause. Pause. Pause. "Really, Anna, let me join you!" "I'll be fine, not to worry!" Anna said in the chirpiest and happiest of tones. GULP. So he relayed the name of John Rosselli's glorious five-story shop on 73rd Street and York Avenue (alas, now gone).

An hour passed. NOT a word. Then two. Bilhuber stared at the phone. Finally, the call. "Hi Anna, how'd you do at John Rosselli's? Her reply, "I took one step out of the elevator, saw lamps, lamps, lamps and more lamps. Thousands of them! I decided you were right after all, fled down to the car and sped away." She continued, "Lets stick to you editing everything down to the three best, letting me pick my favorite."

To some, a lampshade is just a lampshade, but in the land of Jeffrey Bilhuber, it's a whole microcosm of form, function, and craftsmanship. Starting with form, a coolie is the preferred shape. It's pitched, with a smaller ring on top (releasing a minimal amount of light) and a larger ring at the bottom (where the light pours outward). In no particular order, the empire, the drum (preferably a "receding drum" an inch smaller at the top than at the bottom is more graceful), and the oval shapes do their jobs elegantly.

Digging deeper into the bin: Chamfered is more architectural with a vertical beveled edge, and a buillot, wonderful on a desk. A double gallery at the base of a shade is effective diffusion for task light, like bedside sconces. And a half shade is enormously successful in a hallway where it must sit up flat against the wall.

Now, let the games begin. Pongee silk, velvet, or hand-blocked cotton? Just depends. Velvet is opaque and moody, with directed light. Silk is translucent, and wants to be shirred or pleated. Cotton can be smocked to produce enormous detail and depth. There will be seams to cover so you might finish with a contrasting tape, and a half-inch ruffle of the same fabric, at the base, will soften the light emitted. And finally, the surprise that peeks out from underneath. A gold washed paper lining reflects a warm cognac glow on a geometric paper yields a surprise bit of pattern.

The options are dizzying which is why most people without a decorator's cache of knowledge wind up with a white paper shade and quickly forget the rest. Ultimately, the level of detail should compliment the investment elsewhere in the room.

PRECEDING LEFT PAGE: **A tabletop easel on the skirted hall console draws attention toward small-scale intimate pleasure, while the mirrored wall reflects back the grandeur of a period staircase and the sparkle of a magnificent crystal light fixture.** PRECEDING RIGHT PAGE: **The abstract crystals of a mid-century Murano glass chandelier take responsibility for moving the house toward a modern resolution.**

OPPOSITE: **Setting the tactile atmosphere of the master bedroom, nineteenth-century flocked paper in narrow widths gets vertical gimp strapwork to camouflage its seams, creating a secondary kind of architecture. Both the milk glass and gilded bronze lamps are invigorated by shades in matching flocked paper and Chinese blue velvet.**

PAGES 88–89: **Persian blue-glass mirror above the mantel carries the modern conversation of the bedroom where, at the eleventh hour, the furniture plan was rearranged to accommodate a diminutive Maison Jansen writing desk as well as an important Josef Hoffmann Viennese chair. The decadent, sheared-wool hooked carpet begs for bare feet.**

PREVIOUS SPREAD: **Lowering the apple green liner of the bed's corona into our sight line, is an irreverent wink. However, the real triumph belongs to the John Vesey bedside table. Its malachite slab top and stainless steel legs riff on eighteenth-century Louis Seize forms but are madly original. The paintings are by Tim Rollins and K.O.S.**

OPPOSITE: **Doors made of mahogany—incidentally the most stable species of wood to take paint—are given several coats of oxblood color with ebonized paneling. An abalone chair, with opalescent pearly inlay, acts as visual connective tissue to the mid-century chandelier in the hallway.**

OVERLEAF: **The wonder of the dressing room lies in the shimmering quality of frosty light reinforced by silver-leaf wallpaper printed with chinoiserie branches, as well as in the reflection of the gold-washed floor-to-ceiling mirror. Striped festoon shades do their job while looking deliciously like ribbon candy.**

Beauty and function go hand in glove.

Every home has a practical set of needs: deeply comfortable seating, a pleasant place to eat and sleep, ample lighting, and somewhere to stash the stuff of life. In a condensed Manhattan footprint, maximizing closet space is priority number one. Rather than installing a traditional walk-in with a rigorous program of rods and white shelves, Bilhuber opted to remodel a spare bedroom and scheme a lavish dressing room concept instead. A private inner sanctum that aligns with the sybaritic tone of the rest of the house—a ravishing room where the homeowners could emerge refreshed and well-dressed.

To capture all the linear square footage available, an exotic Coromandel screen was repurposed into a twelve-foot long closet by laying its panels flat and retrofitting the inside to accommodate the requirements of hanging and folded clothes. The ingenuity of using a screen as cabinetry fronts is a clever device to enhance beauty and surprise, and to reference back to the show-stealing trompe l'oeil screen painted in the living room's bay window.

The screen's black lacquered design with intricately incised and carved embellishments is a splendid juxtaposition with the Mona Bismarck-inspired chinoiserie branches printed in thick persimmon on frosty silver leaf walls. Taking it one step further, a swoon-worthy gilded chair covered in blue silk damask sits off to the side, completing a tableau of luxury. Form may follow function, but fantastic never looked this fabulous!

OPPOSITE: **A subdued flat weave, camel-colored Wilton carpet, while marvelously sybaritic, settles the foundation of the room, balancing its shimmer with a nuanced foundation.**

OVERLEAF: **The lengthiness of the dressing area called for a linear storage concept; thus the exotic decision to transform a Coromandel screen into a closet, is actually a practical choice. Silk damask fabric on a burnished gilt chair takes the scene right over the edge.**

LEFT: **The television room, paneled in a sycamore wood grid and furnished with a mid-century arm chair, correctly moves the period townhouse along its evolutionary path to the present tense.**

OPPOSITE: **There isn't a homeowner out there who doesn't want a place to put their feet up. A low International style sofa in ivory sheared wool, emphasizes comfort, and an upholstered ottoman in front reinforces it.**

OVERLEAF: **The unexpected presence of a perfectly diminutive lady-like desk, with a beautiful bronze d'ore gallery edge, cleverly expands the function of the breakfast room.**

PAGES 104–05: **Blurring the lines of luxury and practicality, the elegant breakfast room covered in de Gournay paper and featuring a Karl Springer lacquer parchment table and Muriel Brandolini portiere curtains, services sophisticated entertaining, but also stands up to everyday family requirements.**

CLEAR
AND
CONSISTENT

The stringent spirit of Federalist architecture guides the interior designer's choices on this project completed nearly ten years hence. The stone house is nestled in an ancient and bucolic property near Kent, Connecticut. As if all that land weren't enough, it abuts the Macedonia State Park, borrowing its protected landscape as additional scenery. Crisp interiors exude the purity of the surrounding environment, the timelessness of nature and unadulterated simplicity. The homeowners have added or subtracted from the art collection over the years—a passionate pursuit—while the decoration is extraordinarily intact from its original installation. Studying the rooms of projects past is enormously valuable to confirm that their original intentions endure—a "value engineering" of sorts. The decorator excitedly describes revisiting the property recently, picking up the pace on the front walk, past the clipped yew hedge, and anxiously opening the front door for the first time in many a year. Once inside, he felt invigorated (of course!). All the foundations were true and accurate. Just as he remembered, the installation was a wonderfully blurry line where history and modernity mash together.

But better yet, the homeowners were able to contribute their own voice. The platform built by Bilhuber so many years ago, was in fact ameliorated by the homeowner's own life force within it. His clients' passion—collecting contemporary art—allowed the house to evolve in a perfectly organic and personal direction as new pictures and sculpture were added or subtracted to the original scheme. The house now possesses a rich depth that could only arrive in due time, with its owners carefully tending to its evolution.

After leaving the house in Kent, Bilhuber was reminded of story where the decorator Henri Samuel was presenting an installation to his client—a woman for whom a soup-to-nuts approach would simply be the only approach that could work. Instead, the net results of their collaboration produced a beautiful shell—exquisite carpets, handmade curtains, upholstery, and lighting—but it begged for a secondary layer of personality. The woman frowned, "but where are all the personal things—little decorative bibs and bobs, there isn't even a little painting or drawing in this room?" Samuel responded, "Madame, I don't *do* those. That's your job."

While that approach doesn't quite track today, there is of course truth to it. Homes need to reflect the person living in them, and while the decorator is the one who channels those reflections initially, the house takes on even more of a personal patina the longer it's lived in. For many in the modern world, one's individuality and identity is often expressed through art, and it is through this very personal expression of a collection that this home endures, more beautiful today, than ever.

OPPOSITE: **Out of respect for the plaster walls, pictures are suspended from bronze metal chains, a practical accommodation for an evolving collection. A twentieth-century rattan bentwood chair sits underneath a contemporary photograph.**

More cake, less frosting.

PREVIOUS SPREAD: The formalized facade of Federal period architecture asserts a powerful presence on the landscape. Built in 1827, the property abuts the Macedonia State Park and Appalachian Trail.

OPPOSITE: Taking the concept of hospitality and dialing it up, an oversized, five-foot-wide tufted ottoman in the stairwell is an open-armed welcome that's imminently practical.

OVERLEAF: Purity of form reigns and is exemplified by a 1930s parchment covered waterfall table positioned to one side of the sofa as much for practicality as well as a foil for monotony. Above the sofa, a Caio Fonseca painting and a graphite drawing on paper by Harriet Joffee is on the right.

Jeffrey Bilhuber is as comfortable doing twentieth-century modern as he is eighteenth-century traditionalism. What might seem a schizophrenic sensibility would better be described as open-minded filtering. While the tableau changes monumentally from client to client, as it should, there is still continuity in craftsmanship, quality and originality brought to every project. You can never be bored or uncomfortable in one of Bilhuber's rooms.

Rising to the challenge of simplicity is harder than it seems. Everything counts. There is nowhere for a dissident piece of furniture or off-paint color to hide. A tempered environment means every decision has tremendous impact. The historic Federal architecture of the Kent, Connecticut, house wanted a streamlined interior, and so did the homeowners—too much color and complexity wouldn't quite track given the austerity of the setting. The first gasp of, "WOW!" escapes when the front door opens and a cranberry colored ottoman heroically announces the mood: Bold Simplicity! The super-scaled ottoman not only empowers the serpentine staircase that surrounds it, but it is hospitable, as entrance halls ought to be. Throughout the house, sculptural forms animate one another. The apron and stretcher of a Queen Anne bench in the living room reiterate the wave of a rustic coffee table next to it. There is a feeling of less is more. An economy of frill. As much as Bilhuber loves his decorative details, tassles, and trim, this is his hand, tempered. Less frosting, more cake.

Martha Washington, meet Cedric Hartman.

The conversation that might take place between a Martha Washington chair and a Cedric Hartman metal lamp goes something like this:

Cedric: I couldn't help but notice your shape—strong, yet feminine. I adore older women, how old *are* you?

Martha (blushing): Ahem . . . I am lady! And much too old for you."

Cedric: Age is just a pointless, modern construct. If we could have dinner together, I think you'll find I'm quite discreet and that we actually pair well together.

Martha: Well, you are fit. And, quite sexy. Why not?

With its reedy architectural shape, it's no surprise that the revolutionary lamp designed by Cedric Hartman back in 1966 has remained a favorite for Bilhuber over the years. Its slender profile is at home in traditional environments, solicitously hiding behind a sofa or an armchair, just as much as it belongs in the modern landscape. A terrific lamp to read by, it does just what it needs to do, without making a big fuss of itself. For this, and many other reasons, you can actually go visit it in the permanent collection at the Museum of Modern Art in New York City. The Martha Washington chair, sometimes called a lolling chair, associated with the furniture maker Lemuel Churchill, dates back to the Federal period, 1790–1815. This rigid silhouette is one of those old-fashioned frames that is often overlooked in favor of more dynamic shapes like Chippendale or Sheraton. However, that is a mistake. It is distinctively strong, supportive, and even a bit androgynous, imparting American history to any room it sits in.

PREVIOUS SPREAD: Somehow just a drop of vital teal blue on the sofa is all the color required in a gloriously monochromatic room. Crisp basalt trim and chalky plaster walls, along with concise furniture forms, move the restrained plotline forward.

OPPOSITE: Since nineteenth-century Federal houses have historically low ceilings, oversized scale changes help build a modern appreciation. In this case, a large zinc bucket courageously forces the perspective. Hanging on the wall, a Japanese indigo colored patchwork quilt, stitched together with fragments of fabric, is so artful it almost looks like a collaged cityscape. Meanwhile, on the floor, a Martha Washington chair holds court with her attendant, a Cedric Hartman lamp.

OVERLEAF: A commodious demi-lune banquette at one end of the living room acts as a cul de sac, tucking you into the predominant feature of the room, the bay window. Two tilt-top tables reflect the tavern-like experience. One is an original, made of burled elm with marquetry top, and the other a faux bois painted replica.

Modernity is not about a new material, it's about how you navigate your way through the world.

Man Ray, in response to an interviewer who stated that his work was ahead of its time, answered aptly, "No, that's wrong. I am not ahead of my time, I am of my time." To be modern, is to understand the world that surrounds us.

Every so often, Bilhuber will pronounce, "There is newness in everything I do." Being in his time is germane. The canon of Bilhuber projects all attempt to reflect the society we live in, invigorated through history. Rooms have a riveting conversational patter because we can identify our shared past, but history is merely a bridge for expressing what is precisely *today*. Bilhuber's most modern interiors look that way because they are perfectly on cue. The decoration is responsive to the environment it inhabits, but completely unique in the world.

Walking into a book launch at Jane Stubbs shop, Stubbs Books and Prints, then located in a two-room gallery on East 70th Street in Manhattan, Bilhuber opened the door for his date, a current client, impeccably dressed in a tight *rubber* frock. The decorator Albert Hadley, already in the packed salon, edged his way across the room to greet his friend Jeffrey, "Hey baby, what's new!" The young designer focused Mr. Hadley's attention toward his client's dress, "Isn't it fantastic?" Nod of approval. "Look closely, it's rubber." The older decorator examined the dress like a surgeon, and after a quick pause, shouted, "Rubber? *Rubbah!* Rubbah's the satin of the next millennium!"

We should always approach the world with a fresh set of eyes. Fun fact: Bilhuber used to teach a course at Parson's about this very subject: looking around and finding new resources. Though he no longer teaches that course, he is still as wide-eyed as ever, approaching life optimistically. "I'll never stop being curious. It's who I am. I will immerse myself in every aspect of research until I'm satiated." Wherever Bilhuber's investigation leads, it will certainly be filed for later and re-introduced in the form of a new fabric, a new technique, or simply dusting off something forgotten.

OPPOSITE: It's not easy to be both of this time and timeless, but that hard won tension reaches its zenith in the dining room. Perhaps it's the compositional mix of raw elements—polished leather, English walnut and painted pine against a dense and moody matchstrike colored wall—that is just simply something you could look at forever. The oil on canvas of a bird in flight is *Sheer Joy* by Karla Gudeo.

OVERLEAF: A simple sensibility is often the most powerful. Originally the front of the house, this was the double parlour with fireplaces at either end. After an aggressive renovation removing all ornamentation, the room was stripped down to its essence and converted into a dining room. Exploring an American tavern vernacular, the double dining tables accommodate modern needs by encouraging both intimate, everyday use and scaled-up, country weekend entertaining.

OPPOSITE: **These rooms are designed to delight from multiple perspectives. It's not until staring down into the coffee tabletop in the bedroom, that one registers the composition of concentric pinecone petals.** RIGHT: **Moving away from the obsidian core of the house, the palette gets lighter. Mineral colored walls break rank, signaling a new space. The photograph above the mantel is *Converging Territories #15* by Lalla Essaydi.**

OVERLEAF: **The master bedroom's airiness, in the newer wing of the house, is meant to lighten the mood. While staying true to the overall asceticism of design, there is an indulgence of comfort and warmth.**

OPPOSITE: An installation of lacquered red shirts in the hallway by **Jill Weinstock** is linear perfection above a long sheepskin covered bench.

RIGHT: A boxy rattan woven headboard is the vehicle for three bullnose-edged pillows whose classic **70s** shape samples from the **Halston** era, effectively cutting the austerity with a touch of plump voluptuousness.

OVERLEAF: In the eaves of the attic, raw space is carved out for an extra bedroom. The **Turkish** double cushion headboard, a **Bilhuber** hallmark, pairs seamlessly with a sculptural **T-back** chair doing double duty as a bedside table.

A HISTORY OF IDEAS

This project—an incomparable Elizabethan house in San Francisco—involved a herculean feat of engineering. A massive sandblasted glass and iron skylight—the most prominent feature of the house—was dismantled and reinstalled one floor up in the ceiling of the attic. Steel beams were introduced. Brow mopping was involved. It was heroic. Moving the monster was a calculated choice made jointly by the decorator and the architect and mobilized by the clients' resolve to re-claim unused attic space.

Bilhuber—who had given the bottom floors of the house the head-to-toe treatment a few years before—had been called in to see if the top floor had possibility. After touring the large, raw space, literally accessed by a pull down ladder, the decorator set about icing the cake. The renovation (moving the glass skylight and reconfiguring the architecture) and subsequent decoration of the attic was to be the final glorious act in the beautifying of the San Francisco house. The design upstairs had to be as inventive as the design downstairs. The attic rooms could not be perceived as secondary, they had to retain their distinct character and add to the story.

In order to reinforce a consistent vernacular, color saturation was critical. A burst of damask fuchsia on the walls in the gallery bridges the upstairs downstairs scheme, while a cheetah carpet which also runs through the lower halls was laid out wall to wall. Elsewhere, the symmetry and heft of twin console tables skirted in a lush print show Bilhuber's deft touch with pattern and volume. Even the walls of the stairwell are wrapped in an explosive Motherwell-esque digital graphic that can be seen from the floor below. This phenomenal wallpaper installation is like a siren tempting you up the stairs. Not a chance you aren't going up there.

San Francisco has a history of nurturing new ideas. Iconic rule breakers like Tony Duquette, Michael Taylor, and John Dickinson were all decorators from the area whose influence was felt keenly by Bilhuber while working on the project. "It's a town that has historically explored inventiveness," says the designer. "I simply wanted to live up to and build on that tradition."

OPPOSITE: **The second floor mezzanine, one floor below the renovated attic rooms, has a breathtaking plaster bas-relief design of lily pods and sea urchins that are covered in platinum and silver leaf by Dana Volkert. Since the skylight sits above, the carved bits are animated all day by a glorious shaft of light poring into the core of the house.**

Rooms influence the culture around them.

"Rooms have an impact on society," explained Albert Hadley to a young Bilhuber, "You must photograph your work and share it. People will learn from what you create." In other words, a good decorator carries the responsibility to contribute to the cultural dialogue as much as any fashion designer, writer, or film director affects what we think about and how we dress. American style is interesting in that, unlike French or English or Indian or any other country that subscribes to a certain set of cultural constraints, it has had the freedom to invent itself from scratch, without being burdened by history. We have been able to import conceptually and physically from other cultures, while simultaneously cross-pollinating different historical periods to produce a distinctly American point of view.

In one Bilhuber project alone, you may find Turkish headboards and German Expressionist furniture mixed with American hooked-wool rugs. You will never see a strict English country room or a twee French salon since the decorator is liberated to push further and does so on a daily basis. Bilhuber loathes the bandied-about term "eclectic," certainly overused these days to describe a sort of everything-but-the-kitchen-sink aesthetic that's "fun." When his clients invoke the term, they invariably mean an interior that is an enlightened mix of cultures and periods—eclecticism—that has become a touchstone for American style, more than even traditional, modern, or ethnic.

The fashion designer Valentino has an accumulation of astonishing European houses and gardens, all of which have been well documented in books and magazines. All those abodes in glamorous places made Bilhuber wonder why the designer was constantly in New York. What, besides work and meetings, was the allure of our gritty cityscape that kept tempting him back? Valentino's response, "New York is the city that the twentieth-century gave the world." The attraction of American style has nothing to do with copying the refined beauty of eighteenth-century France or hijacking the head to toe exoticism of a Moroccan salon. It is simply about freedom of expression and the liberty to reinvent ourselves along the journey. You'll notice throughout this book, an incredible variety of styles presented—all speaking for their time, in their own way.

PAGES 134–35: **The central picture gallery would have been a thin production if Bilhuber had not raised the decorating bar as high as it could be raised. Sticking to the same elevated vernacular as on the lower floors, walls are upholstered with fuchsia damask fabric, luxurious cheetah carpet runs wall to wall and periwinkle blue trim identifies the room's crowning glory: a gigantic sandblasted glass and iron skylight which was moved from the second floor to the third during the attic's renovation by Butler Armsden Architects. The circular balustrade, installed where the skylight used to sit, allows blue-ish diffused light to penetrate the interior of the house.**

PRECEDING SPREAD: **One of a pair of skirted console tables that flank the colored glass doors establishes symmetry, balance, and order.**

OPPOSITE: **Framing pictures, photos, and drawings with differently sized, antique or period gilded frames, hung from the top down, further appoints the gallery.**

LEFT: **Look closely: a Victorian hooded wing chair is given a full dose of the Bilhuber treatment with two different upholstery fabrics, plus an intricate apple green tape border affixed with small and large nail heads.** OPPOSITE: **Bilhuber knew the door to the study would remain closed most of the time so he installed Moorish inspired, Persian stained glass in a brilliant blue color to enliven the scene on both sides.** OVERLEAF LEFT: **An historical Mauny block print wallpaper, the same as in Bilhuber's New York breakfast room but used to different effect (see pages 60–61), contributes to the grand exploration of mixing styles and periods in the same room. The painting is a seminal oil on canvas by Hans Hofmann.** OVERLEAF RIGHT: **"Every great show needs a 'hook' to grab its audience," says Bilhuber. The electrifying Motherwell-inspired graphic wall covering in the stairwell does the trick perfectly. The black-and-white pattern was procured online from Getty images then altered by Bilhuber's digital tech and printed onto wallpaper.** PAGES 144–45: **The polished chrome and glass propeller coffee table has a chic 1970s snap about it, "but the best thing about the coffee table is the sofa," laughs the decorator. The stunning Greek mattress style form is filled with horsehair that stabilizes the body and keeps the cushions stiff—very important in a room that gets a lot of traffic.**

The charismatic community organizer.

Humble but not shy, card tables have been an irresistible spot for everyone in the room to gather round for years. In fact, that deceptively simple, diminutive table surrounded by four chairs, provides most of the motivation required to even step into a formal living room. Position a card table near the fireplace or window, set it for supper and you'll be amazed at what joy this produces for your guests. Some houses revolve around this unexpected note of practicality because it takes the pressure off a formal dining room arrangement. Even the most glorious eighteenth-century marquetry tables offer an intimacy that's challenging to achieve in a grand space, allowing family and friends to experience a wholly different dynamic in rooms that tend to dictate a prescribed ritual.

Originally meant for cards, the table is the perfect fit for a Sunday lunch for three, just as much as it is a comfortable spot to quietly read the paper with coffee and toast. It's where you go to power up a laptop and read emails as well as being the destination for a Monopoly marathon with the kids. There aren't that many pieces of furniture that can do *that* much for us.

It retains a nostalgic pull from our first association with it: the familiar collapsible metal leg and vinyl topped version that Grandmother would drag out of the closet every Tuesday and Thursday night for bridge parties. Mother inherited that table and would cover it with a tablecloth and have dinner with the family in the television room to watch a special program. Those old fold-down card tables tap into sentimental territory reminding us of cozy evenings at home. And they are *still* useful to have tucked away for *any* occasion. In the modern era of open plan kitchens, infrequently used dining rooms and living rooms suffer from slow or no traffic, but a card, or games, table tucked into a corner of one of those lonely spaces can transform not only the room, but the daily life of the owners, drawing them out of the attention-hogging kitchen . . .

A dutiful cheerleader, Bilhuber has been deploying games tables in projects ever since he hung out his shingle as a decorator. He would argue that every home ought to have some version of this hard-working piece which is not only useful in living rooms but also in the dining room as a smaller "satellite" table. Whether it's a sleek twentieth-century ivory lacquered Karl Springer number, an old-fashioned English mahogany carved beauty, or the ubiquitous Ikea Parsons table, there are few excuses not to find the perfect match. When shopping for your new best friend, one rule of thumb is to slightly scale up. Thirty-nine inches square performs better than thirty-six—even three inches can make a big difference. If space is tight, one of those terrifically engineered console versions that sit against the wall can accommodate any expanding or contracting social situation just by rotating out a gate leg and flipping down the top.

Capable of adding to the purpose of any room that it inhabits, the charismatic games table is one of those rare creatures in the decorating world that manages to provide pleasure, beauty, and function all at once. It may sound over-reaching, but any piece of furniture that can do all that and more, is well worth the price tag.

OPPOSITE: **Electric blue side chairs fitted with handy back handles for mobility are a contemporary counterpoint to the exceptional Maltese cross shaped games table in polished mahogany. All of Bilhuber's projects feature at least one games table.**

OPPOSITE: **The winning trifecta of mass, saturated color, and eye-catching detail is unleashed everywhere in the family room. Here, a Tony Duquette moment starring a malachite resin console table, apple green combed plaster walls, a buttoned turquoise and amethyst armchair, magenta corduroy ottoman, and eighteenth-century ivory porcelain.**

OVERLEAF: **The family room is an expertly handled balance of color. Three shocks of red—one on the settee centered under the window and a jolt on each corner banquette at the opposite end—help to thread the jewel toned palette throughout the room. A pale lacquered ceiling is passive while still being active.**

PAGES 152-53: **A strategic floor plan is essential for a long room up in the eaves. Low banquettes maximize sloped space in the corners and a clementine lacquered wet bar with a polished bronze frame and monumental amethyst slab handles, tucks into the niche carved out of a dormer window.**

Always push the boundaries. Knowledge is advanced by opportunity.

Fabric is a tactile thing of wondrous beauty that makes Bilhuber's heart beat a little faster. It's obvious the decorator is enthralled and enchanted with every aspect of the life of a textile—from who designed it and where it is loomed, straight to the workroom where his designs are sewn. It's a mutual admiration society made up of artisans he adores, supports, and nurtures, who ultimately support him (and his clients, who benefit from "exclusives" crafted just for him) right back.

With an alchemist's hand, he somehow tackles the *most* complicated and daring mix of prints. Imagine these in color: A cotton paisley batik on a tufted armchair, a massive block-printed geometric on a sofa, another contemporary paisley used in two colorways on the same chair, traditional floral chintz throw pillows tossed about, a silk Fortuny armchair in another corner, solid velvets and suedes covering more chairs, ottomans, and banquettes, then weave in a few footstools dressed in entirely different patterns and put that all together in the same room. Not easy and not for amateurs—there are rules that if you know them, can be broken, but if you don't, it could wind up a flat out expensive disaster. Registering a room like this will defy your preconceived boundaries and expectations of "what goes together." This is shocking at first, but eventually the jolt of newness is processed and finally accepted into a new decorative vocabulary. Then, suddenly a similar daring mix shows up in other pictures of other rooms by other decorators in design magazines and all over Pinterest. That's how the zeitgeist works. A new idea is tough to swallow and then it's all anyone is drinking.

Bilhuber will fixate on a certain fabric and want to revive its popularity. For example, "The caress of wide whale corduroy! We've forgotten how luxurious . . ." he goes on, "I remember getting my first brown corduroy hip hugger pants. I loved them so much, you had to cut them off of me!" Sure enough, you can bet wide whale corduroy memos will be rounded up out of the vast fabric resource library at his design studio, new examples called in from fabric vendors and suddenly there it is: a pair of tufted cherry red wide whale corduroy corner banquettes, the star in a room of fabulous fabrics, looking so completely fresh you think you might need to run home and recover all of your sofas in it too. Why not? In the wise words of the decorator Angelo Donghia, "You should feel at all times that what is around you is attractive . . . and that you are attractive." If fabric assists in that tenet, then release the swatches.

OPPOSITE: **The dormer structure is referenced rather than disguised by bisecting the periwinkle French lacquer walls with vertical trim. Recessed ceiling lights are camouflaged with vintage brass artichoke fixtures.**

OVERLEAF: **With no shortage of pizzazz, the office still maintains an appropriate sobriety. The silk velvet on the sofa and chair is in shades of pomegranate, which settles the cool tones of the walls. Japanese stone paint brushes are part of the owner's curated collections.**

Feeling safe and comforted is an excellent way to end the day.

Life is charged with a fair amount of challenge outside the home and occasionally inside, too. But at the end of the day (or sometimes all day) what could possibly beat stretching out in bed? Maybe one or two things, but really, shutting out the noise and retreating to the inner sanctuary, whether its packed with children and dogs or stacks of reading or a new boyfriend, is the single, most fantastic luxury. The other rooms in the house are very useful, but a bedroom is a kind of temple.

Canopies, coronas, testers, and half testers are a hallmark of Bilhuber's work. You'll see them in practically every project. It's his mantra that the bed should bring great comfort to the person using it and a bed that fully envelops you in fabric is a means to that end. It's impossible to find a bedroom in the entirety of the Bilhuber collection that isn't treated as a cathedral to comfort.

For him, it all started with an insider-y, to-the-trade-only, textile purveying duo called D.D. and Leslie Tillett. Those names had been on the tip of Jeffrey Bilhuber's tongue since day one. Mrs. Kennedy had splashed their Carnation fabric all over the White House, Bunny Mellon commissioned yards and yards of silk-screened panels and pennants for Nantucket, as well as other patrons with exceptional taste like Parish Hadley, Billy Baldwin, and Brooke Astor who lined up to put in orders. Bilhuber jumped at the first chance he had to use Tillett in a project, "a canopy with that kind of fabric obligates you to look at it!" Of course, there are hundreds of other fabrics out there that receive the Bilhuber canopy treatment as well, but the breezy American vitality and astonishing range of pattern of Tillett continues to have a path beaten to its door by the decorator. Whether or not, the entire bedroom is covered in fabric or just the bed, "canopies are a terrific mechanism to feel safe and comforted," Bilhuber says, "as if everything is going to be just fine, it really is."

PRECEDING LEFT PAGE: **Any image dreamt up or imagined can be achieved with a digital graphic, in this case the pattern is wildly exaggerated: perfectly normal poppies expand to sci-fi "poppies from Mars."**

PRECEDING RIGHT PAGE: **The vintage 1930s double sinks work a strange kind of magic with the 1980s style mirrored mosaic. Together they help you to forget the bathroom doesn't have a window. Who said it even needed one?**

OPPOSITE: **A sumptuous and nuanced guest bedroom, completely covered in a made-to-order printed canvas from Tillett Textile.**

OVERLEAF: **Museum-worthy side tables are prototypes from a seminal modernist architect. The ceiling is lacquered in the palest lavender shade. The silk-screened pattern on the walls extends onto the tufted headboard, which expands this room's footprint.**

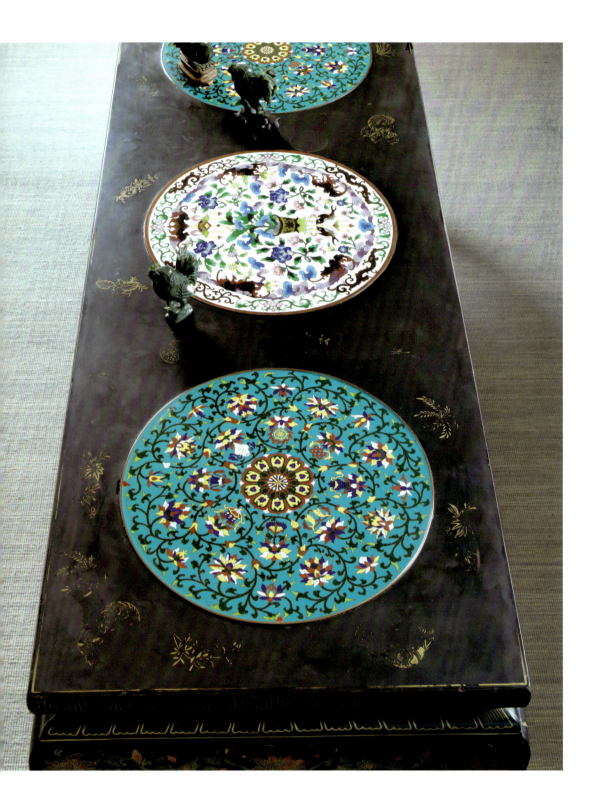

PRECEDING SPREAD: **Bilhuber, the mix-master of fabric and pattern scores with a sophisticated palette used experimentally.**

LEFT: **Cloisonné plates inlaid into the coffee table top smack of Doris Duke's ethnically inspired home Shangri La in Hawaii.**

OPPOSITE: **The dramatic skylight beckons visitors from below.**

166

BETWEEN HEAVEN AND EARTH

Over the course of a decade collaborating together, Bilhuber and the homeowners had developed a sort of decorating shorthand. The designer could visualize exactly what the homeowners meant when they tossed out identifiers like "playful and optimistic" or "soothing and restive" at brainstorming meetings.

What Bilhuber had created in their previous residences was something tender and romantic, but now it was time to excavate his clients' inner urbane, adult selves. This new house was a beautiful bright white canvas, but it didn't arrive without its own set of challenges: a previous renovation that removed most of the interior walls on the first floor had the unintended effect of blurring the living room with the entrance hall, rendering both spaces moot.

The first order of business was to find a mantel and restore the sanctity of the living room as a family hub for gathering. The decorator found the perfect one: a dramatic, polished chrome mantelpiece. That shimmering hearth clearly articulated what the designer wished the house to express about his clients: gorgeous, glamorous, and all grown up!

A vast plane of inset mirrors straddling either side of the chimneybreast creates the illusion of enormous front-to-back windows, optically transforming the square footage of the room. The absence of a front hall meant that the staircase occupied a visual connection throughout the entire house. In response, Bilhuber folded them into the decorative decisions with equal weight: the entire staircase, from ground floor to rooftop was lacquered in a bold shade of peacock blue and the treads were upholstered in a Wilton carpet the same color.

The remainder of the house was given a modernist color blocking treatment. The overall effect is blue skies and bright sun and a world filled with goodness. A delightful suspension of place, where you are cushioned between heaven and earth, where tomorrow might possibly be even better than today.

OPPOSITE: Adding a modernist lift to an old-fashioned tufted form, this glamorous 1960s Billy Haynes sofa is meant to walk the red carpet, or in this case, a black lacquer floor. Meanwhile, the unexpected location of the sofa—up against the balustrade of the main stairway—expands the perimeters of the narrow living room in which it sits, cleverly including the peacock blue painted staircase as an arresting visual component, as if it were destined to be the center of attention all along.

OVERLEAF: Since the living room is lean, employing bulky upholstery would have consumed valuable space, and the 1930s Japanned armchairs are the epitome of a chic, urban resolution. With enough mass to almost be categorized as settees, the caned arms and backs provide an element of translucency allowing the room to breathe. Floor to ceiling mirrors flanking either side of the chimneybreast double the enchantment, reflecting polished black floors and a purposeful bookending of bright Persian blue punch.

I'm not a decorator, I'm a magician!

Indeed, it can be enough to fill a house with comfortable places to sit and pretty things to look at, but a master puts on a show. And a good show is all about timing, rhythm, syntax, and narrative. The white rabbit doesn't prematurely pop out of the hat while the audience is still checking their coats, the magician waits until every last person is seated, works the room for a few beats, and then—abracadabra—white rabbit, or in the case of Jeffrey Bilhuber, dazzling, reflective *mirror*. And not just a pretty one over the mantel—that would be amateur hour—the magician knows that the unexpected surprise of inset reflective panels flanking the fireplace, floor to ceiling for fourteen uninterrupted vertical feet and, continuing up onto the ceiling are going to be a transformative experience for the audience. Never seen that before in a living room? Precisely.

For Bilhuber, the road to glamour is paved with mirrors. Perhaps it began with Halston. His long friendship with the designer included regular Sunday night suppers featuring elegant, but simple fare like Chicken Pot Pie, Blanquette de Veau, and Bollito Misto served by his affable butler Mohammed at that famously documented townhouse, 101 East 63rd Street. Grey wall-to-wall wool carpet in the step-down living room, enormous flannel sofas, constellations of twinkling votive candles on every surface, a forest of specimen white orchids, and mirror—lots of it, reflected back the modern American dream. In the mid 1970s, it was all daring and bold, and palpably sexy. When a new look is being established, anything is possible. And, what's sexier than possibility?

When the young decorator invited the legend over for dinner at his own "mini me" apartment, the evening was anticipated with some measure of nervousness, "What would Halston think?" Eager to swank it up, Bilhuber went out and bought as many white Phalaenopsis orchids as the tropical rain forests could produce and artfully jammed his apartment with at least a few dozen: "I lit so many candles that the oxygen in the room simply evaporated." Handing Halston a drink, he queried, "Sooo, whaddya think?!" Halston's reply, "More mirrors." Of course, what else? From senior magician to apprentice, the notes were basic, "More pizzazz and polish. Be bolder, cleaner, simpler. More."

It's tempting to reduce sleights of hand like running a mirror up a wall and onto the ceiling as mere trickery, but go ahead and try it at home. Doesn't quite look the same, does it? That's because there is a complicated narrative built up around it, woven throughout the room and the house, supporting the punch line. It's about mastery and skill. Transforming nothing into *something*. It was the great American designer, Albert Hadley, who at the very beginning of Bilhuber's career decreed, "Never forget! You're not a decorator, you're a magician!"

PRECEDING SPREAD: **An intoxicating assembly of color is confident enough to carry the couture narrative; the portiere curtain and upholstered furniture swathed in ink blue, mossy green, purple, and persimmon look like an Yves Saint Laurent runway show, while black lacquer appoints the double front doors with importance.**

OPPOSITE: **A blue portiere curtain hanging at the right of the double doors architecturally delineates the front hall from the living room, making every entrance a grand one. Tactile comforts take a front seat in the main salon where a pine green cashmere throw quietly awaits discovery on the back of a matching armchair. Another blanket, in bright persimmon, boldly asserts itself on the purple gauffrage sofa.**

OVERLEAF LEFT: **A stunning painting of dancing red stars by Pierre Marie Brisson radiates joy and modernity, while the gleaming chrome hearth, one of the first acquisitions for the house, anchors the living room in glamour.**

OVERLEAF RIGHT: **A great table will inform anything that surrounds it and this scalloped-edged coffee table happens to be one of those benchmark pieces. Beautifully articulated with a verre eglomise top and ivory inlay, its hexagonal shape is easy to navigate.**

It's powerfully important to sit at the table and *talk* to each other.

Yet another casualty of twenty-first-century living, along with quaint corner shops and small houses in the 'burbs, is the vanishing dining room. Often surrendered in favor of a sleek screening room or maybe even a billiard's parlour, homeowners prefer to avoid lighting the candles in an unused room that gets dressed up twice a year. It seems that when we eat together at all, it's rapidly at the kitchen island or passively in front of a screen. Despite the casual, multitasking path we are going down culturally, most Bilhuber clients tend to keep the sanctity of the dining room ritual intact, as it should be, possibly because their decorator has strongly urged them to do so!

Regardless, a beautifully appointed dining room, whether modern or traditional, is obviously a platform for civilized behavior and sparkling conversation—an opportunity to stretch discourse and use the good crystal and china. The decorator, a fan of eating meals from a proper plate with the nice, but not 'good' silver laments, "I can spot the family who doesn't eat meals together from a hundred paces." Most of us don't have time to gather together every night, but we can certainly manage setting the dining room table once or twice a week for a special lunch or supper. The benefits of that weekly observance could transform the dynamic of a family's habits.

Splendid dining tables abound, but Bilhuber is a pushover for the center pedestal version, "Nobody wants to spend the evening straddling a table leg!" Furthermore, the decorator insists that a proper dining table is worth the cost, "I promise, it *will be* a family heirloom," adding, "I've never had a client that wasn't re-using a beautiful old inherited piece or whose grown children aren't all clamoring for the contemporary one they are sitting around at their parent's dinner parties."

The real luxury in this life is to commune together, reinforcing our family relationships and expanding the table to include neighbors and friends. Really, the defeated dining room ought to be resuscitated, but even if it isn't, a corner banquette in the kitchen or a card table in the living room will do just fine. The point is to connect with each other over a meal, a jigsaw puzzle, a deck of cards, or good old-fashioned conversation.

PRECEDING SPREAD: Bilhuber deftly carves out space for formal dining by positioning a handsome William IV mahogany pedestal table in the available square footage between the open plan living room and adjacent library. Dining chairs are pulled away and lined up against the mirrored wall, allowing the table to perform double duty as a grand surface for a spray of forsythia. Dense ink blue walls in the library signal a change of purpose, brilliantly acting as a hyphen between the dining and media areas.

OPPOSITE: Vintage button back dining chairs keep their original olive green leather upholstery, while a rogue white-painted armchair breaks up the set.

OVERLEAF: A staggeringly beautiful French nineteenth-century mahogany and ormolu gondola shaped sleigh bed begs for odalisque reclining. The daybed originally sported a mattress covered in zebra stamped cowhide that Bilhuber shanghai-ed in favor of obsidian colored velvet—a strategic decision to enhance the beauty of its form rather than draw attention to its upholstery. Curtains are heavy-weight custom-dyed linen interlined with sound-proof felt, and they completely enclose the media room on either end. Naturally, the outward facing drapery is a contrasting satin fabric, rather than linen, of the same blue color. When closed, the silky shine reflects the swanky vocabulary of the living room.

PAGES 184–85: **Sought after French ceramist Roger Capron devoted his life to the art of tile collage. Low to the floor and pleasingly staggered, a 1960s pair of ceramic coffee tables are expansive enough to accommodate books, *objets*, and even cocktails in the cinema room.**

PRECEDING SPREAD: **The term "ombré," and its process, have cross-pollinated from high art into the satellite worlds of fashion, beauty, and decorating. Like in the paintings of Ed Ruscha, ombré animates light and shadow, competently camouflaging mass—in this case, a dense twelve-foot long sofa. In order to appreciate order and symmetry on either side of the sofa, the center is intentionally thrown off with irregularly sized velvet throw pillows in an original combination; two twenty-three-inch squares, an eighteen-by-twenty-one-inch oversized lumbar, and a small twelve-by-sixteen-inch lumbar. Hanging above, an Andrew Saftel painting attracts attention against Persian blue moleskin walls.**

OPPOSITE: **If a runner were rolled straight up the middle—with either side of the treads bared—the stairs would seem stingy. Instead Bilhuber cleverly expands their width with a visual illusion. Employing lush peacock blue Wilton carpet installed flush to the diagonal stringer on the right, the carpet is installed up the left side as a standard runner would be, exposing a bit of the riser and tread painted in the same exuberant hue.**

OVERLEAF: **People tend to think bedrooms ought to be warm, but Bilhuber will generally opt for frosty therapeutic tones of blue and green because "the coolness allows you to settle" and the coziness comes from the act of actually pulling up the covers. Here, the master bed is dressed with sybaritic fur and decorative pillows as if it were furniture for lounging on, rather than something straight out of the bedding department. Bedside tables are opportunities for extra storage; a pair of 1940s mirrored chest of drawers responds with practicality and glamour. Mementos and art, including a Sally Mann photograph hanging above the owner's collection of amethyst crystal orbs, personalize a private space.**

It's easy to get white wrong—it takes talent to get it right.

"The first of all single colors is white . . . We shall set down white for the representative of light, without which no color can be seen; yellow for the earth; green for water; blue for air; red for fire; and black for total darkness." —Leonardo Da Vinci

The power of any palette has everything to do with how the color is arranged. Consider the difference between the paintings of two masters of chromaticity, Mark Rothko and Ellsworth Kelly. A Rothko, with it's dense blurring color fields that vibrate the longer you stare, is like a thumping living heartbeat—it absorbs the light—and becomes a sort of neutral, no matter its hue. While Kelly's paintings, which engage the viewer with form, shape, and color, use white as an absolute, forcing you to acknowledge bright green or acid yellow or pure black. Now translate those two different approaches to the canvas of a home. It's important to insert here that approximating either a Rothko or a Kelly on your walls is close to impossible, but that's not the point anyway. Rather, the takeaway is that walls painted with dense viscous hues à la Rothko neutralize because there is no point of contrast, thereby encouraging a wholly different feeling than rooms with vivid color that are connected by glacial white.

Bilhuber strategically launches both types of color campaigns throughout his work. In the case of the Manhattan townhouse featured in this chapter, white is a modifier for the deployment of fearless color. White isolates the exclamation point of radiant yellow in the kitchen, ink-y blue in the library, and pine green, amethyst, and persimmon in the living room. Non-color causes us to sit up and acknowledge those bright gifts. White renders everything surrounding it crisp, clear, and united. There is nothing boring about it; in fact, it's unadulterated and simple white that allows the true modernity of a space to come to the fore.

PRECEDING LEFT PAGE: It's important to add graphic clarity to a liquid palette. Small black and white framed photographs by Masao Yamamoto, to the right of the master bedroom television, suggest a visual wake up call.

PRECEDING RIGHT PAGE: Counterintuitively, Bilhuber introduces proper furniture into the bathroom environment. Upholstered chairs with heart-shaped backs—beloved heirlooms from the owner—cut the travertine and tile tension with a sweet note of softness while the cotton Indian block print shade allows for light, ethereal pattern, and privacy all at once.

OPPOSITE: Looking much like a bubble that has floated to the top of the stairs and landed on the wall, a gorgeous multi-colored Klari Reis glass sculpture is animated by light pouring down from an overhead skylight.

OVERLEAF: You wouldn't want to see a Tuscan farmhouse kitchen in the middle of this sophisticated narrative, so instead sunshine yellow, streamlined cabinets, and crisp white countertops reflect big city glamour, reinforcing the polished design credo of the rest of the house.

PAGES 198-99: A pair of basket-front sideboards by mid-century design star Edward Wormley are an alternative to built-in cabinets, allowing the kitchen to function as a casual dining room.

A NOBLE APPROACH

Hay Fever is the kind of cobbled-together-over-the-centuries, charming country house that sits in our viewfinder as a snapshot of in-between-ness. The house is snagged in several time periods with evolutionary clues revealing themselves around each corner. Original foundation stones were laid in 1668 for a two-room house that became a Quaker boys school, a tavern, a printing house, the village museum, and a rambling inn fabled for its mature specimen trees and fragrant gardens. The building eventually morphed into its latest and final incarnation as a residential home, updated with contemporary fixes every hundred years or so by various owners.

Situated inside the village of Locust Valley on Long Island, the house presents a facade that clearly echoes the architecture of George Washington's Mount Vernon—a rather pleasingly symmetrical asymmetry. The right side is seventeenth century, the middle portion with twelve-over-eight windows is eighteenth century, and the six-over-six fenestration on the left side is nineteenth century. Finally, the crowning achievement was the addition of a raised roof in the latter half of the Colonial Revival period.

One is reminded of *noblesse oblige*, the responsible stewardship of what has preceded. Imposing order on the landscaping, the grounds are laid out classically, with lovely quadrants and pea gravel paths. The two outbuildings were joined at the turn of this century by esteemed Palm Beach architect Maurice Fatio to situate around an interior courtyard.

Hay Fever's rooms are informed with a romantic sensibility, but rather the Proustian version of romance—a waft of something enchanting that lingers in your memory forever. The more you look the more you discover. Amazingly, this very American house was a test of competence for the designer who needed to prove he was as capable in this vernacular as any. He threw himself into period research, rediscovering the protagonists of the era: the power of rich colonial red and the decadent sparkle of hand-cut crystal. It was very much about seeing the artistry in things that had always been there, but with new eyes. Wherever Bilhuber's hand falls he is going to bring great beauty, but it's when he is stretching his reach that his full potential is unlocked. It's quite admirable to walk the difficult path when you are at the top of your game—and Bilhuber wouldn't walk any other.

OPPOSITE: The nineteenth-century Native American lithographs, part of the three volume collection *History of the Indian Tribes of North America*, were originally commissioned in 1821 by Thomas McKenney and James Hall to document a vanishing culture, though a fire at the Smithsonian destroyed most of the originals. Bilhuber first spied the portraits at the Pierre Hotel apartments belonging to Yves Saint Laurent and Pierre Bergé, designed by a very young Jed Johnson.

OVERLEAF: The original foundation stones layed in 1668, just forty years after the British bought Manhattan from the Native Americans, have expanded over the centuries to allow several new wings that wrap around an interior courtyard.

Establish a sense of arrival.

Great designers know the story starts the minute you pull into the driveway. The approach must be two things: tempting and unambiguous. Green architecture acts as silent tour guide, leading you gently into the experience. Stepping out of the car at Hay Fever, you find yourself on a structural path of crumbs, laid out by the decorator, directing your momentum. Transitioning from the urbane vernacular of New York City to the bucolic calm of the countryside, Bilhuber aims to transport you.

The garden's vision is distilled through a few perspectives. A clear acknowledgement of Colonial Revival hierarchy is first established with an orderly carpet of green grass and formal boxwood in the Jeffersonian style planted in the front quadrant of the house. The outlying gardens are contained chaos with utilitarian raised beds for growing vegetables and flowers. The exterior hints at what the interior experience might be, building anticipation and fueling excitement. There is no chance that once you've pulled in, you won't immediately feel you have arrived someplace quite special. You want to know more, to dig in! It's the first course to a glorious meal.

PREVIOUS SPREAD: Leathery green English ivy covered obelisks rise up out of a striking chartreuse groundcover, Lysimachia nummularia "Aurea." Concord grapes (the only grapes indigenous to North America) are trained on the arbor over the master bedroom wing.

OPPOSITE: The last time document paper, Climbing Hydrangea, appeared in an entrance hall was during *Gone with the Wind's* pivotal burning of Atlanta scene. It was re-created for Hay Fever by the indefatigable John Knott at Quadrille.

OVERLEAF: The main artery of the house, the reception hall, is occasionally and appropriately used as a serving room for casual dinners at home, and is the ideal spot for a small nineteenth-century Regency-style mahogany sideboard.

PAGES 210–11: When passing through rooms at Hay Fever, it is not uncommon to travel through different periods in American history as well. Balancing the formality of the turn of the twentieth-century wing of the house, Bilhuber responds with order and symmetry, arranging chairs, lamps, and crystal girandoles in pairs around a slipcovered console table finished with two horsehair tassles on either end.

If you take care of something, it will take care of you.

On the eve of hosting a dinner party, a client's wise mother advised, "If you don't have time to clean the house, at the very least clean the mirrors and crystal." Bilhuber concurs, "If that's all you've got time for, it's time well spent!" Preferable to a one-time swipe of the crystal, the decorator recommends developing a deeper maintenance list revolving around things that need to happen in order to keep a house breathing. Like cleaning the windows at least once a year. That single day of effort will positively affect the other 364.

It's really about taking responsibility for what you have and being a decent steward. One morning after breakfast on a weekend trip at Martha Stewart's place in Maine, Bilhuber was searching high and low for his hostess—peeking in the living room, the kitchen, her office. No Martha. At last he found her, unsurprisingly, in the laundry room. There was our symbol of American domesticity—a woman who has crafted an empire on elevating housekeeping—in an unobserved moment, taking care of the chores with pleasure and pride. "It is a testament to Martha's integrity," says the decorator, "It's lovely to witness someone in full accord with what they have."

While laundry is sort of a *must*, why not repair that broken furniture that's been sitting around forever? There are workrooms that have maintenance departments, places devoted to re-gluing broken legs and arms, tightening frames, and touching up surfaces. Go there and get to know them. For about three hundred dollars, your lovely chest of drawers can be cleaned *and* restored, which will help maintain its value significantly.

Bilhuber often speaks about using the fine things every day, like linen and silver, and how it can positively change the rhythm of life. Why keep it locked away? Sterling silverware is a cinch to clean if used frequently: toss in soapy water on one side of the sink, rinse on the other, dry, and put away. Keep all the other silver polished too—you wouldn't let your teeth go un-brushed would you? And please, vacuum the lampshades every six months with a dust buster, as it will preserve the life of the material. Polish the brass switch plates, if you've got them. Think about it, they get touched *a lot*. Every once in awhile, take your feather pillows outside and beat the dust out. You'll stop sneezing so much. To easily get rid of odors, leave a big bowl of sliced lemons in water on the kitchen table overnight (a post-installation trick ensuring the client arrives to a citrusy clean house).

If you are lucky enough to have a housekeeper, let them know what matters to you. The bed ought to be made how you like it! Photograph exactly how much top sheet fold-over you prefer, how the pillows should be arranged, and keep it in a house maintenance book. Obsessive, maybe, but if you like things done a certain way, then everyone will be happy. The impact of a house well run is everything. Snap polish and pizzazz doesn't just happen. You have to nurture it.

PREVIOUS SPREAD: **The dense sitting room diorama is bifurcated by historical apple green above the dado and essex green below and is finished with a French blue-and-white decorative trim border whose goal is to engage all four walls visually. Humble monk's wool pulls across the middle add privacy and warmth while the more ornamental block-printed chintz stays fixed on the sides.**

OPPOSITE: **On the mantel, nineteenth-century Henry Northey Hooper girandole candlesticks, whose chaste scenes of provincial farm life contradict the glamour of refracted light in their cut crystal prisms.**

The C word.

She flung herself full-length on the stage, drummed with her feet and, taking the corner of a small Persian rug in her teeth, worried it while I sat rigid and appalled on the sofa, pressed against the chintz cushions.
—Alec Guinness

Wherever chintz winds up, performing on the stage with Sir Alec Guinness or poured onto everything in a Billy Baldwin bedroom, it always brings a backstory with it. It's simply a very narrative fabric associated with waspy-ness. What better place for it to wind up then pulled strategically throughout the rooms of Hay Fever, on the very waspy North Shore of Long Island. Appropriately chic and comfortable, its floral pattern allows the garden to find its way inside. In the drawing room, the decorator chose a more masculine iteration of glazed cotton Le Lac (a hand print from the collection of Maison Hamot in Paris) on the curtains and upholstery, fitting for a man's country house. In the Monticello yellow cloakroom, throw pillows are covered in Hazelton House (and appropriately named "Petworth"), beautifully hand-printed with astonishing scale and color. In the bedroom, a bit of vintage '40s glazed cotton chintz can be spotted on the sofa. As explanation for the quiet riot, Bilhuber simply says, "The house asked for it."

Chintz has been in fashion since the 1680s when the European rage for "glazed calico," as it was known, kept the mills in India humming. Since then, every era has produced greatest hits from small scale riffs in the '60s to the English beaten-about varieties liberally used during the reign of the superb decorating firm of Colefax and Fowler to being slightly abused in the '80s with its too-much-isn't-nearly-enough approach. It's just one of those historical fabrics we return to again and again because it speaks volumes.

Today chintz is so deeply immersed in our vernacular, dragging its old-fashioned values around with it, that the topic is actually approached with caution. "It's a terrifying conversation to have with clients," Bilhuber laughs, "the mere mention of the C-word can clear an entire room." The challenge is to tell a new story. Add to that the simple fact that hand-blocking a print in twenty colors by no means connotes anything close to the word chintz, as in "cheap" or inexpensive. This is a cloth that is so justifiably expensive you have to lie down on the (chintz covered) sofa when you first get the bill!

Who better to redefine world-weary chintz with than Bob Pittman—a veteran risk taker responsible for introducing the world to MTV and redefining radio programming at iHeartMedia. When Bilhuber decorated Pittman's beautiful old stone house facing the reservoir in Katonah, New York, he convinced his client to recast the C-word in an entirely unique way. He proposed using the *backside* of a densely saturated pattern for curtains. Only when the sun hit the fabric, would that familiar chintz pattern ghost through. A modern trace of a floral, used in reverse, ingeniously connected the Federal house to its past while simultaneously moving it toward its future.

PREVIOUS SPREAD: A grandly florid 1940s hooked round rug is startlingly dramatic on ebonized floors. But the charm lies in the myriad of details, like the bullion fringe hanging from the mantel and a symmetrically hung collection of silhouettes.

OPPOSITE: Formality without the tedium—the captivating tableau includes lacquered papier-mâché deer head trophies with shed antlers mounted above Imari plates and a pair of blue opaline vases, part of a larger collection of French glass, wildly popular in the mid-1800s, during the reign of Napoleon III.

LEFT: **By placing mirror around and above doorways, the eye is fooled into thinking the proportions of the door openings are greater than in reality. A very Sibyl Colefax thing to do.**

OPPOSITE: **Named for its shape, the High Low sofa was designed with languishing in mind, and is, of course, the napping spot of choice in the sitting room.**

OVERLEAF: **The point of this library is to retrieve books and read them—preferably horizontally—somewhere else. A waist-height banking table, brought in from the Matinecock Bank when the Phipps family closed the Locust Valley branch, is the only furniture in the room.**

Red!

We are all familiar with libraries and formal dining rooms swathed in deep crimson, but red for a bedroom, very unexpected. The exceedingly rich master suite at Hay Fever has a vivid nineteenth-century perspective that conjures up a touch of Newland Archer's world.

Not shy at all, red elicits emotion. Energy personified, it's the primal force running through our veins. We are made of it—and drawn to it. Before the nineteenth century, when synthetic dye was invented, getting your hands on a foot, a meter, or a yard of red fabric would have been impossibly rare and costly. The dye was extracted from crushed insects called cochineals, small bugs living primarily on cactus in Mexico. In fact, when the Spanish arrived in the 1500s, cochineal became the major export to the Western world, winding its way into the parlors of the highest echelon. In France, Madame de Pompadour coveted her hard-to-get red so much so that she covered practically everything in it, from expensive velvets to everyday chintz.

Without a doubt, vivid red is the star in Hay Fever's master bedroom. What makes it less scene-stealing is that it happily shares the stage with white. Like a glass of water for the girl who drank too much, crisp refreshing white is the sobering agent. If you've ever stared at pictures of the monumental library at Charles de Beistegui's Chateau de Groussay, the second thing you notice after the opulence, are the white slipcovers. They are wingman to all that poshness. Same tactic used here—an expanse of white fabric on the inside of the bed canopy and on the tufted headboard moves these rooms into our modern radar, fearlessly.

PREVIOUS SPREAD: **A room that manages to be both civilized and amusing is an accomplishment. A strategic furniture plan helps; rather than centered, the formal dining room table is to one side and sitting room positioned on the other.**

OPPOSITE: **A pair of "cousins"— almost matching 1930s American flat back chairs look like they are whispering in each other's ear. Vivid red acanthus leaf fabric is applied directly to the walls, without padding, to give texture in a way that paper cannot.**

OVERLEAF: **The scene-stealing master bedroom is dominated by a canopy bed whose hangings are operable. The carpet is a fine example of hand-woven Scottish ingrain or flat weave, and increasingly rare to find as original.**

PAGES 230–31: **A grand gesture, tempered; the rich red linen canopy is lined with swaths of refreshing white fabric. This measuring technique is a surprisingly English notion, where massive canopy beds were ornate on the outside and puritanical on the inside.**

PAGES 232–33: **This is the last place you would want to hang a landscape, rather something with a presence that forces you to stay in the room. Positioned above the mantel and mounted in a period gesso and gilt frame, an historical print by J. Whitehorne, *The United States Senate Chamber*, circa 1842, is stern and engaging.**

ADVENTURES OF THE WHITE SQUARE

OPPOSITE: A polished steel biomorphic coffee table shatters notions of what a coffee table should be, and presents itself as a sculptural object of enormous sensuality and sensibility.

OVERLEAF: Furnishing the boxy shaped living room with a circular sofa centers the activity in the middle rather than a traditional boxy layout in front of the fireplace. The sofa frame is upholstered in cocoa colored suede and the cushions in amethyst silk.

PAGES 238-39: Like a mechanical wheel, the segments of the sofa are designed to rotate toward the warmth of the fireplace or the view outside. The round carpet further reinforces the idea of circulation. Four rivet-like standing lamps illuminate the perimeters of the wheel.

Slashing through the scripted presumptions of ski lodge glamour—like wall-mounted stags' heads and hauntingly abandoned criss-crossed snow—a boldly modern vacation home sets a new mountain vernacular. Located within the village footprint of the burgeoning town of Aspen, the exterior presents as a slightly ersatz yet charming turn of the century Victorian cottage, but when the front door opens, a crisp geometrical arrangement of lines announces an entirely new thought process of what these interiors should be. The home is connected by a series of provocative artistic moments, suggesting Bilhuber's design decisions are driven by the homeowner's intellectual curiosity and willingness to embrace the piste less traveled.

A gently curving cypress wall, inspired by the arc of a Richard Serra installation, directs family and guests into the airy, double-height living room. Floating in the center of that room, a segmented round sofa—which brilliantly rotates toward the fireplace or the slopes depending on which view is more seductive—anchors the inventive ski house design.

Bilhuber's commitment to maximum beauty with only the most essential elements, echoes the simple complexity of nature. Frosty white plaster walls conjure glacial peaks, while plenty of stone, iron, and bronze evoke earthier elements. There is a lean athleticism to the interiors: strong silhouettes cut muscularly through the space, leaving room for the client's contemporary art collection to be fully appreciated. You can't help but to be swept up into the International style optimism of rooms whose economy of expression functions totally on point, without sparing a bit more.

OPPOSITE: **The heroically scaled graphite and paper sculpture by artist Jae Ko hanging over the fireplace visually connects to the engineered steel and timber bridge on the left and to the mechanical shape of the sofa wheel—a flawless fit of art, architecture and design.**
RIGHT: **The mid-century pedestal table, whose dense top feels weighty enough to hold court with the mass of living room upholstery, engages beautifully with a polished bronze sculpture by Bernar Venet.**

OVERLEAF LEFT: **An International style oasis in the storm, the modernist addition to the late nineteenth-century Victorian architecture is timely and appropriate, and reinterprets the modern goals of a seasonal and year round ski lodge.**
OVERLEAF RIGHT: **Like a train chugging through the Alps, white painted plaster walls are the appropriate backdrop for the blackened steel architecture of the suspension bridge that connects the guest wing with the master bedroom.**

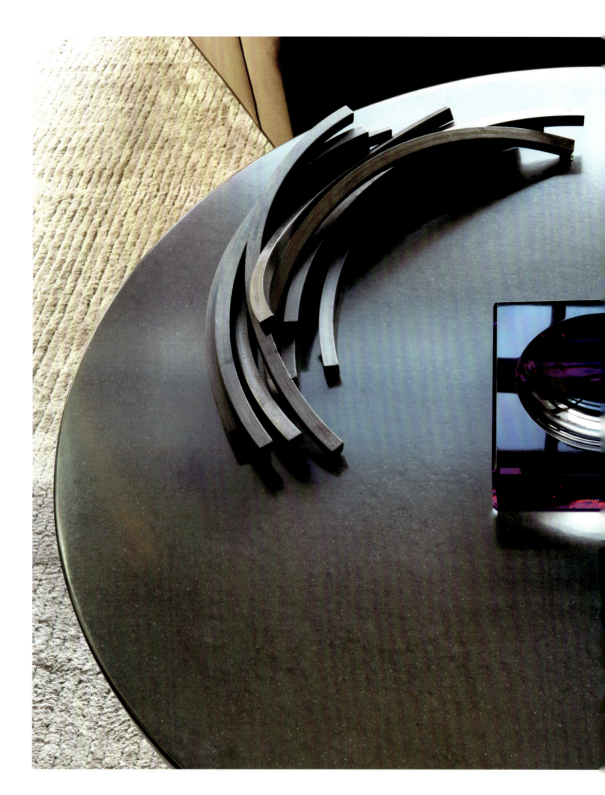

Architecture is the
structure of beauty.

"Sometime around my twelfth birthday, I discovered a splendid Edwardian casket in the attic completely filled with dozens of my father's, his father's, and his father's brother's sketchbooks of charcoal drawings. *Amazing* renderings of Elizabethan and Tudor buildings, gothic fragment studies and other remarkable portraits, landscapes, and botanical sketches," remembers the decorator. Rifling through pages of architectural studies, the young Bilhuber glimpsed an artistic thread in his DNA, and felt a remarkable connection to his family.

Sanctioning his creative impulses was gratifying; "I wasn't really productive until I was using the key component of who I am." As noted by poet e.e. cummings, "It takes courage to grow up and become who you really are." While Bilhuber's father had been an engineer for Mobil Oil, his every breath focused on mechanics, his grandfather had been the Head of Engineering and Experimentation for Steinway Pianos (he died with 18 important piano patents credited to his name, most notably in 1936, he designed a sound board that revolutionized Steinway's Upright offering, by tilting the frame and strings to allow for longer string length, which provided the same optimal "Grand" tone and quality that made the Steinway brand famous, at a more affordable price), and both of their lives had been consumed with making forms function.

Robust decorating must always respond to structure. "Architecture is the stimulation," explains Bilhuber, "the design choices that follow are self evident." The inside of a project is dictated in large degree by its shell. That said, some of Bilhuber's most interesting work arrives in the absence of a shell where he has the freedom to draw outside the lines. It doesn't hurt that the decorator has always been a frustrated architect, a perpetual student for whom researching the components of a building's composition is as high on his list of amusing things to do as scoring at the auction house. He speaks the lingo fluently, and can't help himself: resolving door openings or repositioning a stairway to the other side of the room simply because that's where it always should have been and no one had the ingenuity and insight to insist it be moved there.

Recently Bilhuber was thrilled to hear his own architectural sentiments echoed while observing the first grade carpentry class at his son Christoph's school. "The boys were learning how to think their decisions through," he noted. The concentration required of the linear process began with a critical conversation about the integrity of structure and how it is *never* random; you don't just start gluing pieces together, but rather good structure (structure that stays standing, rather than collapsing) is a pre-determined process from the first saw cut to the finished product. "Life's essentials laid out clearly!" Bilhuber exclaims, "First grade is fantastic!"

OPPOSITE: The unusual heft of the custom lacquered steel table helps it to stand up to the hunk of arching cypress wall. Flat art pops up out of Wendy Babcox book and is the perfect three-dimensional object in the simple tableau.

OVERLEAF: The heavy duty slab top, granite base, and thick steel shaft of the table in the foreground express volume as does the massive dining room banquette which is broken down with intermittent wide bands of different colored horsehair. The iconographic Austrian chair references chalet style and helps to reinforce the mountain vernacular.

Tension builds drama.

"You can't see a line without a curve," Bilhuber explains regarding his motivation for the project in Aspen, "the round shape of the sofa in the living room *forces* you to notice the room's linear architecture." In other words, the decorator aimed to push the tension between shape, color, mass and texture to the limit. In the dining room, a contemporary light fixture explodes against the white walls, reinforcing the negative space around it. In the entrance hall, a triangular console courageously asserts its heft against the curve of the cypress wall behind it and downstairs in the family room, an amorphous coffee table covered in mirror-like shards lands with a glamorous thud on the soft wool carpet. In a sense, these are bright stars of their own individual galaxies. This is Bilhuber triggering our awe with a few, rather than many, glorious statements.

Site-specific sculpture, where an artist has been commissioned to fit something into a prescribed setting, is art reacting to its environment. In fact, the art wouldn't exist without the environment. For Bilhuber, the Aspen project was an exercise in expressing the strength of a form while emphasizing the positive and negative spatial relationships around it. The simple goal of decoration is always function and beauty first, but beyond that, to facilitate an appreciation for the environment in which it sits. Leaning into a more post-modern approach in Aspen, the net result is a pleasing friction between object and setting.

OPPOSITE: **Like a frozen lake in the middle of the forest, the glass topped table was absolutely necessary to offset the weight distributed around the perimeter of the room. A phenomenal "Agues" light fixture designed by Lindsey Adelman is suspended from the glistening flaked mica and quartz ceiling.**

OVERLEAF LEFT: **Natural beauty; majestic snow covered Aspens loom large in the silent landscape.** OVERLEAF RIGHT: **A digital graphic in the powder room centers you at the polar vortex of a winter wonderland.**

The envelope please . . .

Wallpaper is a lovely idea and one that has been kicking around for centuries. The Middle Ages hung expensive tapestry over the cold stone of their drafty castles for practicality as much as narrative beauty. When European tapestry shipments dried up in the 1500s due to an embargo from the Catholic Church, English ingenuity produced hand-blocked wallpaper. At first, these papers were a grand affair meant for public spaces and palaces, but by the eighteenth century the English and French aristocracy were obsessing over flocked papers and exotic scenics for their own homes. Once wallpaper became mass-produced in the twentieth century, it was used as an inexpensive way to add beauty and dimension to rooms that benefited from a bit of something *more*.

Bilhuber has been a lifelong booster of wall coverings, pursuing new material and technologies, while at the same time just as enamored with ancient techniques. In fact, every chapter in this book presents a range of examples from period papers to scaled-up digital supergraphics. It's stunning to compare the effect a traditional Mauny print from Paris has on the Edwardian breakfast room chez Bilhuber (see pages 60–61) versus the exact same print tempering the totally twenty-first-century happy modernism going on in a San Francisco stairwell.

The intention of patterned wallpaper, like the one used in the guest bedroom in Aspen, is to keep you focused on the interior by defining its perimeters—to cosset and hold you in the room. Conversely, the purpose of a scenic paper is to open up a magnificent view and create a transporting experience. In between that, there are a myriad of ways to add architecture and hide flaws and simply wow the viewer. Just walk into a room hung with a Mauny mural or any de Gournay hand-painted Chinoiserie and you will be agog.

PRECEDING SPREAD: **A cheeky reference to fur boots and ski hats, chairs in the primary guest bedroom are covered in graphic pony and sheepskin.**
OPPOSITE: **Love in a cold climate; a traditional Farrow and Ball paper tucks you right into the cozy guest bedroom while sculptural Sputnik-esque table lamps provide the edge. A superb sketch by George Condo accelerates the room into the modern age.**

OVERLEAF: **The master bedroom is painted an unexpected pale lilac amethyst—a heavenly antidote to the staggering white view straight up the side of Ajax mountain seen out of the corner window. The large oil on canvas painting is by Howardena Pindell.**

LEFT: **Splendid details like a frosty opaline lamp and textural Raku pottery lend depth and dimension to the master bedroom.** OPPOSITE: **Intended to soothe and immerse, a Turkish headboard gets a pale linen and silk velvet hand-stenciled in gold paint, while the bed is dressed with flattering shell pink linens. The three-dimensional installation above is by Jacob Hashimoto.**

OVERLEAF: **Under a banner of clouds, two chunky headboards tether the bedroom to terra firma. A cubist bedside table with cone vase plays the same melody heard throughout the house, that of sculptural forms carving shapes in space.**

LEFT: The family room downstairs is given over to the pursuit of ping pong. The graphic painting is by Cordy Ryman. OPPOSITE: A biomorphic coffee table enforces contemporary panache in the downstairs family room, insisting that rec rooms need not sacrifice a bit of style. Nick van Woert's delightful picture *Dreamcicle* looks on, half interested, half not.

OVERLEAF: So that everyone can watch the daily foosball match, Bilhuber folded in auditorium seating that doubles as bunk room. The mattresses are dressed for lounging in tailored orange wool corduroy.

A moveable feast.

Many of Bilhuber's clients are prodigious fine art collectors. "It gives me great comfort when a homeowner is intellectually stimulated and passionate about art they love," the decorator says, "it's a strong indicator we will be productive together and the house will project their curating just as much as mine." Inevitably clients' collections expand and contract over the years: a painting in the hall might migrate into the bedroom to make way for the next new thing, for example. This hierarchical rearranging works because even long after the decorator has finished up the job, he has made calculated decisions in advance to accommodate just that kind of growth of personal expression. Houses are never meant to be static, rather more evolutionary and a personal art collection is a wonderful way to chart growth.

Sometimes a blank wall is just fine too. At one of Bilhuber's completed projects, there remained an enormous swath of empty space where the client was still searching for something telling, appropriate, and likewise phenomenal to anchor the room. The client's choice to leave the wall empty for the next few years was quite an admirable one; her confidence as a collector superseded any shred of insecurity that her house might appear "unfinished." Ultimately, she decided to have Bilhuber install the screws into the wall so that each time she passed by that spot, she'd be reminded that something *eventually* had to hang there. It longed to be completed and eventually was.

Another example of Bilhuber's ingenuity was recently witnessed in an enchanting Colonial Revival house high in the hills of Seattle. The owners had begun to build on a splendid collection of twentieth-century paintings and photography. As the works were being hung during installation, a few large pieces were still being considered and taken on approval. A large canvas over the primary sofa in the living room was ultimately returned and the hunt continues. Between now and the time that the "room-making" painting is located, Bilhuber encouraged the owners to relocate a brilliant Arshile Gorky painting from another location in the house. "Don't hang it on center. It should be just a few inches off to right of center and slightly lower than expected. It wants to *feel* that it's in transit, and that adds to the human qualities of the quest." Decorative art, as opposed to fine, is an equally valuable part of the discussion; both have enormous merit but ultimately function differently. While the former is meant to provide backdrop and beauty and to assist the decorative decisions, fine art is more of an academic pursuit that when displayed, insists the viewer pause and catch his breath. "I draw a hard line in the sand between the two conversations," the decorator says, "although both can serve a true purpose when placed in capable hands to bring value and reason."

OPPOSITE: **Vik Muniz's *Pele* is a fitting tribute for an athletic house.**

OVERLEAF: **Artist Jose Davila's amazing collection of work is hung asymmetrically forming a precise square and illustrating the success of positive and negative space.**

266

Afterword

COTTON TO GOLD

If you give me the basics, I'm going to make them better. I will always address universal truths and build upon them, bringing value to the conversation. The work my firm does will always be symbiotic with my clients' goals: comfort, suitability, and creativity. These are our goals too … but my job is to add more.

A final story before you go. One day, back when my dear friend the inimitable designer Halston was earning his keep as an in-demand milliner, he was up in his atelier fitting a client with a headpiece. For the grand finale, he wrapped a length of grosgrain ribbon around and around, criss-crossing the material over the woman's head and finishing it with a tight, meticulous bow that concluded an effortlessly chic and modern look. "It's the most beautiful thing I've ever seen!" the client shrieked, "How much do I owe you?" Halston replied, "That will be fifteen-hundred dollars." Frowning, she said "Fifteen-hundred dollars? It's only a ribbon." He walked back toward her, "That's where you're wrong," he said and carefully unwound the entire thing, placing it in her outstretched hand. "*Now* it's only a ribbon."

The ribbon was the "basics"; that's where every project starts. It's what we do with those basics that translates a collection of furnishings and appointments in any home into a language that is transformative. It's my very own brand of alchemy. I will spin whatever you put in front of me into something much more glorious than you ever imagined without me!

First published in the United States in 2015 by
Rizzoli International Publications, Inc.
300 Park Avenue South
New York, NY 10010
www.rizzoliusa.com

Copyright © 2015 Jeffrey Bilhuber

Designed by Doug Turshen with Steve Turner

2015 2016 2017 2018 / 10 9 8 7 6 5 4 3 2 1
ISBN: 978-0-8478-4596-5
Library of Congress Control Number: on file

Printed in China

Acknowledgments

In writing *American Master*, I am reminded of the astonishing human and creative resources that surround me. As I enjoy success at the top of my game, I know that I am here because of the support provided by the heroes in my life. Confidence, razor-sharp focus, and experience define the people to whom I am most indebted, but ultimately it's their unshakeable trust and loyalty over time that matters most.

Mariska Hargitay and I have collaborated for twenty glorious and productive years. The most worthwhile creative partnerships are the ones that extract your very best. Mariska and her husband **Peter Hermann** are a thoughtful team that have *always* pushed me to new places without ever sacrificing an ounce of joy along the way. Her selfless commitment to end domestic violence as Founder and President of Joyful Heart Foundation is exemplary of a woman who gives her all to her family and craft, and then gives even more to the community that surrounds her. We have both excelled in our respective professions through discipline, hard work, and commitment, fusing fearlessness and friendship.

The impact of **Anna Wintour** on my life has been significant. When she was looking for a young decorator to spiff up the offices at *Vogue* (back when it was on Madison Avenue!), I was the *chosen one*—handpicked from a rather competitive lineup. Anna found me when few others had, and it was through her nurturing and championing that my credibility as a modern American designer was firmly established.

I stand in awe of my wonderful friend **Martha Stewart**. Beyond her depth of talent and determination, it is her generosity of knowledge which has enhanced many aspects of my life, and the lives of millions around the world. She has shared valuable insights about her innate capabilities in business, the pursuit of beauty, and a cultivation of the land.

Everyone is aware of the influence **Margaret Russell** has in the world of interior design, decorating, and publishing. I'm at a remarkable point in my life where I can reflect on, with great pleasure, how she and I have grown together. Margaret was the stylist on my very first photo shoot for *Elle Décor*. Now at the helm of arguably the most influential magazine in the field, *Architectural Digest*, she's as much fun today as she was twenty-five years ago selecting flowers in the market at 6:00 on a chilly spring morning.

I have had the great fortune of working for a collection of truly **astonishing clients** whose unflinching support has allowed me to soar. As a designer, and as a barometer of change, I want to share my creativity with many. In that vein I am blessed that my clients have selflessly allowed their private homes to be shared, studied, talked about, and enjoyed.

Even before I met **Sara Ruffin Costello**, I was smitten by her smoky beauty and obvious talent as a journalist. When I read her glorious review of my last book in the *Wall Street Journal*, I was in love! She has helped me find the words that were missing to describe my work, and never told me to put a cork in it when I said too much. She has been absolutely essential to the development of this book with her uncanny ability to read my shorthand. Most importantly, she knows when to work and when to play, both of which she does with a full-on passion. She's my kinda gal.

I have toiled alongside revered art director **Doug Turshen** for many moons, creating three extraordinary books together, each one more evolved than the next. It isn't surprising that Doug's calendar is always filled—he is as reliable as he is creative—a notion that also extends to his team which includes the very impressive **Steve Turner**. Steve normally has five to fifty people throwing directions at him on any given day. He is never resistant, *always* accommodating, and has built on our unique vision since the beginning.

I am devoted to the brilliant photographer, **Bill Abranowicz**—one of the very best in his milieu. But more critically, Bill is unflappable! When I asked him to trek up the side of a snowy mountain in a spring blizzard to get *the shot*, he didn't flinch. He has met my high expectations and surpassed them. Bill surrounds himself with excellent people—his first lieutenant, **Jessica Leibowitz**, helped keep things humming while lugging around the Hasselblad camera I insisted we use.

Rizzoli represents the pinnacle of interiors publishing and having the Rizzoli imprint, under the fastidious leadership of **Charles Miers**, is an enormous source of pride. My longtime editor, **Isabel Venero**, has managed to tighten and brighten *American Master* while simultaneously managing to meet the moving targets of our critical publication deadlines. Her clarity and point of view on this project have been invaluable.

Over the course of my career I have sought out and nurtured great talent. I am proud of the accomplished designers that have passed through Bilhuber and Associates—**Tom Scheerer, Steven Gambrel, Thom Filicia** and **Jesse Carrier**, to name a few. I pride myself on being a good teacher, and these were terrific students—best in class, for sure. It's a privilege to witness how they have effectively used the creative and business lessons learned, and applied these to their own considerable careers.

In the last five years I have demanded more of my employees than ever before. I am grateful and humbled to work with a team of professionals at **Bilhuber and Associates** who shore up my everyday with their focus and loyalty. Make no mistake about it: I am tough and very demanding, and to succeed in my firm—which I built with talent and sheer determination—you must work with great focus. The talented people in my office represent the very best in their field, which is why they are here.

Architects build what we only dream about. I have been fortunate to work with many of the country's greats. **Peter Pennoyer, Ferguson & Shamamian, Fairfax & Sammons, Shope Reno Wharton, Butler Armsden**, and **Stephen Sullivan** have assisted me and my clients in designing and building a few of America's greatest houses and apartments.

There is a reason **Connie Plaissay for Plaza Flowers** is the go-to florist for everything involving beauty—whether it's a photo shoot for a magazine or a mega event. Connie's shop, with its brilliant window displays, is a testament to his well-earned success.

Not *everything* is made in New York City after all . . . there are truly wonderful people out there running smaller businesses in little towns and **Peter Flammia at Little Flower House in Locust Valley** is one of them. I am grateful for his skill with flora and his willingness to craft an arrangement of hard-to-find specimens in a "New York minute."

At a certain point in my life, I didn't know what all the work was for—that is, until I started a family. Having my son **Christoph Bilhuber** has been that game changer, and my good life simply got *a lot* better. Watching my son develop and grow over the last seven years and seeing him flourish at school, I realize more than ever the importance of following your instincts, however young you are, and to find your passion. Learn more about what you love, and success will follow. To quote e.e. cummings, "It takes courage to grow up and become who you really are."

Knowing that things are running seamlessly at home has allowed me to do the very best work. Our wonderful nanny, **Jennie Lowry**, has devoted herself to my family and in turn has become part of *our* family. When all goes well on the home front, the days (and nights, and weekends!) in the office are fruitful and productive.

I can count **my friends** on three hands. These trusted few make a core that has consistently been by my side through *everything*. They are my chosen family and I am happy to have them in my lifeboat and comforted that we will continue to grow together.